Nāgārjuna's Seventy Stanzas: *A Buddhist Psychology of Emptiness*

Nāgārjuna's Seventy Stanzas: *A Buddhist Psychology of Emptiness*

David Ross Komito

Translation and commentary on the *Seventy Stanzas on Emptiness* by Venerable Geshe Sonam Rinchen, Venerable Tenzin Dorjee, and David Ross Komito.

Snow Lion Publications
Ithaca, New York

Snow Lion Publications
P.O. Box 6483
Ithaca, New York 14851
USA

Copyright © 1987 David Ross Komito

First Edition U.S.A. 1987

Printed in Canada

Library of Congress Catalogue Number

ISBN 0-937938-39-4

Library of Congress Cataloging-in-Publication Data

Nāgārjuna, 2nd cent.
    Nagarjuna's seventy stanzas.

    Translation of: Śūnyatāsaptatikārika.
    Bibliography: p.
Includes index.
    1. Mādhyamika (Buddhism)—Early works to 1800.
2. Sunyata—Psychology.   I. Sonam Rinchen, 1937-
II. Tenzin Dorjee.   III. Komito, David Ross, 1946-
IV. Title.
BQ2910.S9422K6513 1987   294.3'85   87-9654
ISBN 0-937938-39-4

The author wishes to express his gratitude to his many teachers, without whose kind instruction this work could never have been accomplished, and especially to Helmut Hoffmann, Tara Tulku Kensur Rinpoche, and Geshe Sonam Rinchen. The author also wishes to thank the National Endowment for the Humanities, whose grant of a Summer Stipend was instrumental in the completion of this project.

Contents

Preface   11

Foreword   The Legend of Nāgārjuna's Encounter with the
          Nāgas   17

Chapter 1   Buddhist Psychology   19
Section
1-1   General Comments   21
1-2   Buddhadharma   23
1-3   Perception & Conception   36
1-4   Subject; Part 1: Attention   52
1-5   Subject; Part 2: Meditation   59
1-6   Object   66

Chapter 2   The *Seventy Stanzas on Emptiness*   77
Section
2-1   *Seventy Stanzas Explaining How Phenomena Are
      Empty of Inherent Existence*   79
2-2   *Seventy Stanzas on Emptiness* with Tibetan text and
      Commentary by Geshe Sonam Rinchen   96

Chapter 3   The *Seventy Stanzas on Emptiness* and its Transmission   183

Section

3-1   Treatises by Nāgārjuna   185

3-2   Translation of the *Seventy Stanzas* During the First Introduction of Buddhism to Tibet   192

3-3   Translation of the *Seventy Stanzas* During the Second Introduction of Buddhism to Tibet   199

3-4   Contemporary Translation Activities   206

Footnotes   210

Bibliography   216

Index   221

"Reality according to Buddhists is kinetic, not static, but logic, on the other hand, imagines a reality stabilized in concepts and names. The ultimate aim of Buddhist logic is to explain the relation between a moving reality and the static constructions of thought."

T. Stcherbatsky
Buddhist Logic
Vol. 2, p. 2

Preface

In the summer of 1982 I traveled to Dharamsala, India to do some advanced study on Nāgārjuna's Mādhyamika system with Geshe Sonam Rinchen, one of the scholars at the Library of Tibetan Works and Archives. I had reached a limit in what I could understand about Mādhyamika by merely reading texts, and had a number of questions which remained unanswered. I felt that these questions could only be answered through dialogue with an accomplished scholar who had trained in the venerable monastic tradition.

For some time the focus of my Mādhyamika studies had been Nāgārjuna's treatise *Shūnyatāsaptatikārikānāma*, the *Seventy Stanzas on Emptiness* (hereafter referred to as the *Seventy Stanzas*). I'd begun work on this treatise while a graduate student, translating it under the supervision of Professor Helmut H. Hoffmann and commenting upon it and its relation to the Prajñāpāramitā literature for my Ph.D. dissertation at Indiana University. In this project we utilized the standard commentaries on the *Seventy Stanzas* for guidance. The translation produced at that time replicated the terseness of Nāgārjuna's treatise. In the course of our work together I had learned much about Nāgārjuna's system, but felt that what I didn't know was perhaps even

11

more vast as a result of having learned a title. Frustratingly, there seemed to be few, if any, scholars in the west with whom I could consult who were any better off.

As I began asking Geshe Sonam Rinchen my questions about the *Seventy Stanzas*, I realized that I had finally met a true treasure house of knowledge about Mādhyamika. He had begun his studies at Sera Monastery in Lhasa, Tibet, fled in 1959 to India with about 100,000 other Tibetans and completed his scholarly studies there, finally obtaining his Geshe (Doctor of Theology) degree. His answers to my questions were always lucid, and many difficult points in Mādhyamika began to come clear. Amazingly, when I put questions to him he often asked me which explanation did I want? As he showed me, there were many ways to analyze the subtle points in Nāgārjuna's system. His own preference was to adopt the Prāsaṅgika view of Candrakīrti, as his monastic tradition followed the Prāsaṅgika interpretation favored by Tsong kha pa, the founder of the dGe lugs pa sect to which Sera was connected. I found that this view profoundly enriched my understanding of the *Seventy Stanzas*, a draft of which I had brought with me.

In the course of our discussions we determined that the most profitable way for me to continue my training in Mādhyamika would be for us to read the *Seventy Stanzas* from beginning to end, discussing problems as they arose in our reading. As our reading progressed I began to revise my translation of the *Seventy Stanzas* under Geshe Sonam Rinchen's direction, all the while taking notes on his explanations of the significance of the stanzas (Sanskrit: kārikā(s)). During this process I realized that my notes represented a nucleus of a contemporary commentary on this ancient treatise which reflected both the views of Candrakīrti and the oral tradition of interpretation which Geshe Sonam Rinchen had learned in Sera.

This struck me as being of particular value, and after some discussion we determined to continue our work with the formal intention of actually producing a contemporary commentary on the *Seventy Stanzas* which could be of use to the modern reader. This is also why we did not choose simply to translate the Candrakīrti commentary, for Candrakīrti himself can be extremely difficult for the nonscholar, and we felt that we would have simply found ourselves in the regress of needing to comment upon Candrakīrti as well as Nāgārjuna, leaving the modern reader with a larger task, and perhaps not succeeding in providing him/her with what we had intended to provide: a readable version of one of Nāgārjuna's philosophical treatises.

This desire to serve both the needs of the nonscholar and the scholar also presented us with a problem in translating. The terseness of the stanzas themselves is often very confusing to the nonscholarly reader, and both Geshe Sonam Rinchen and I felt that many other translations of Nāgārjuna's treatises were prone to being inaccurately read, though translated correctly, simply because they were so terse. Therefore we determined to interpolate English words into our translation of the stanzas which are not found in the original text but do reflect the meaning of Nāgārjuna, at least as the Tibetans interpret Nāgārjuna. To preserve the accuracy of the translation we have adopted the device of italicizing all the words in the English translation found in chapter two, section 2-2, which actually correspond to the Tibetan. In section 2-1 the stanzas are presented without italics or commentary. In this way we hope to satisfy both the needs of the scholar for a precise translation and the needs of the nonscholar for a readable and comprehensible translation.

We have taken great care in our work to select English terminology which conforms to the style now being developed at the Library of Tibetan Works and Archives and also which carries the appropriate English connotations. For this I must express special appreciation to Venerable Tenzin Dorjee, the third member of this translating project. Ven. Dorjee is fluent in both Tibetan and English, and has taken pains to develop his command of English by studying English Literature at Indian universities. We spent considerable time discussing the specific English words we wished to use in the translation of both Nāgārjuna's treatise and Geshe Sonam Rinchen's commentary on it, attempting to select English words which had both the appropriate denotations and connotations. This was particularly difficult and yet important. In this respect our translation has the merit of being an accurate reflection of what an indigenous tradition believes the text is saying, and is not merely what western scholarship says the words in the text mean. Those who would prefer a more literal translation may wish to consult either my earlier translation of the *Seventy Stanzas* or else Chr. Lindtner's translation of it. I believe, however, that they will find our translation to be of great help in understanding Nāgārjuna's thought.

In addition to the translation of Nāgārjuna's *Seventy Stanzas*, this volume contains another section, chapter one, which is my own commentary on Nāgārjuna's thought. No Tibetan scholar would attempt to fathom one of Nāgārjuna's treatises without a commentary, but just as significantly, no Tibetan attempting to understand Nāgārjuna would be doing so without the benefit of a monastic educational training. Western readers are not in this position, and I believe that much that Nāgārjuna says seems obscure because the modern reader does not have a context in which to place the treatise. My own commentary is intended to provide this context. To do this I have chosen to adopt the perspective of a Buddhist psychology and to focus on those aspects of Nāgārjuna's thought which could be called "psychological." I do this for several reasons. For one thing, the whole purpose of Buddhadharma is to alleviate suffering, and all Buddhists assert that this is primarily a mental operation, for the root of suffering is ignorance. Indeed, the whole thrust of Nāgārjuna's system is its intended clarification of erroneous cognition. In the west, scientific psychology is the discipline which seeks to alleviate sufferings cause by mental problems. In this respect, the intentions of psychology and Buddhadharma are the same, and so I believe that psychology can serve as a context for translating Nāgārjuna's conceptions and intentions into a form which will be meaningful to the modern person. I hope that I have been able to accomplish this to some small extent by showing how much of Nāgārjuna's system can be understood as a psychology and how this psychology can be of use to the modern person who, afterall, is in many respects faced with the same human problems as were Nāgārjuna's contemporaries.[1]

Finally, in chapter three I locate the *Seventy Stanzas* within the context of Nāgārjuna's other treatises and relate the history of its transmission to us.

David Ross Komito
Stanford University
March 1986

Foreword
The Legend of Nāgārjuna's Encounter with the Nāgas

According to legend, Nāgārjuna was an abbot at the great Buddhist monastic university of Nālandā. He was a great debater and vigorous supporter of the Mahāyāna doctrine, teaching to large audiences in the monastery. At one time he noticed that whenever a certain two young men attended his teachings, the entire area became filled with the fragrance of sandalwood, and when they departed the fragrance disappeared. When Nāgārjuna questioned them about this they replied that they actually were not human beings but sons of the nāga king, and that they had annointed themselves with sandalwood paste as a protection against human impurities. (Nāgas are water serpents or dragons.)

They told Nāgārjuna that in the time of the Buddha the nāgas had attended the Buddha's discourses on the Perfection of Wisdom and that because few human beings had understood the discourses, they had written them down to save them for a time when a human being would be born who could understand them. They invited Nāgārjuna to their kingdom to read those Perfection of Wisdom sūtras, and he accompanied them to their undersea world. After spending some time in the kingdom of the nāgas, Nāgārjuna returned to the human world to teach what he had learned, bringing the 100,000 Stanza Perfection of Wisdom Sūtra with him.

Nāgārjuna took his name from his encounter with the nāgas, and the *Seventy Stanzas on Emptiness* is one of his expositions on the Mādhyamika system which he learned from the sūtras in the keeping of the nāgas.

Chapter One
Buddhist Psychology

Section 1-1 General Comments

Buddhist psychology is a label which can be applied to a complex fabric of systems of thought and practice of some 2500 years duration which is the fruit of some of the best minds of Asia. It is a tightly woven fabric which, if viewed up close, can be bewildering in its complexity. The text which is translated in this book is a treatise which can be likened to a single thread in this fabric. The concepts expressed in this treatise interlock with the concepts in all the other treatises in this fabric and derive their meanings from them. Thus it must be comprehended in dependence on the larger context of the other treatises which form this fabric.

Over the course of this 2500 years of Buddhist history various systems have been developed to describe this fabric and its strands. In principle, any one of these systems could be used as a basis for explaining or describing a single thread, such as our own: Nāgārjuna's *Seventy Stanzas on Emptiness*. Naturally, some systems are better than others because they represent more sophisticated or clearer attempts to reach their common goals. As the *Seventy Stanzas on Emptiness* has for 1,000 years been extant only in Tibetan, it makes sense to approach the problem of explicating the text from the perspective of one of the analytic and synthetic systems in use in Tibet. Even in making this decision many choices are available, for there were numerous systems taught in the Tibetan monasteries where such exegetical activities were carried on.

Although the ancient monastic system of Tibet has been destroyed in Tibet proper, some remnants of it remain in the communities of the Tibetan refugees in India. In particular, the monks of the dGe lugs pa sect have not only taken on the task of carrying on their traditional educational system, but they have also opened it to western students. My exposition depends on what I have learned from them either in person or from what they have written.

This exposition can be grouped into three divisions which structure it and follow the pattern of the traditional psychological notion that subject (consciousness), and object always arise and cease in dependence on each other, and that their functional relationship is what is referred to by the terms "perception" and "cognition."

Following this scheme, the *Seventy Stanzas* itself would be placed in the object division (section 1-6), as would the commentaries on it or collateral to it, because it considers objects or things. Within the subject division (sections 1-4 and 1-5) I have followed treatises based on Asaṅga's *Compendium of Abhidharma* and a variety of dGe lugs pa texts on meditation. Within the perception division (section 1-3) I have followed treatises based on Dharmakīrti's *Commentary to Ideal Mind*. In all cases I have merely summarized those aspects of these treatises which are important for understanding the *Seventy Stanzas* and Geshe Sonam Rinchen's comments on it. I have provided references in the footnotes for those readers who wish to learn more about these treatises.

Section 1-2 Buddhadharma

What is called "Buddhism" in the English speaking west is called "Buddhadharma" in the Sanskrit of the old Indian monastic universities. It is a complex of doctrines and practices which derive their authority indirectly from the experiences of the masters of Buddhist doctrine and practice, and directly from the experience and teaching of the Buddha himself. Indeed, his teaching itself derives from his experience, particularly the experience known as his "enlightenment."

This experience is described in rather flowery terms in the *Buddhacarita*, a text which postdates the Buddha by 500 years, but is based on traditional teachings about his life. According to this text, Shākyamuni, the Buddha to be, renounced the householder's life at age 29 and set out on a religious quest that was marked by ascetic practices and mental disciplines which are generally known to us under the rubric "yoga." The text tells us that he attained mastery of two kinds of yogic concentration exercise under two different masters. Under the first master he attained a state of "nothing at all." Under the second master he attained a state of "neither perception nor nonperception." These, as we will see in section 1-5, were later known as the seventh and eighth dhyāna(s) (concentrations), respectively. The mastery of these forms of concentration did not, however, satisfy Shākyamuni's religious quest, a significant point, for here he breaks with the tradition prevalent at his time which taught that the mastery of subtle states of concentration would liberate one from the sorrows of the world.

Next, he set out on a long fast (as a form of purification), but gave that up as merely weakening the mind. Finally, seating himself under what later came to be called the "bodhi tree," he vowed not to move from that spot until he had attained his goal. Shortly thereafter Māra, a god who is the personification of lust and death, attempted to budge Shākyamuni from his seat, but touching the ground with one hand, Shākyamuni remained immoveable. In an interpretive sense, we may say that the meaning of this tale of the attack of Māra is that having vowed not to move until he attained freedom, Shākyamuni was immediately beset with impulses deriving from his own instincts to live, which were threatened by his vow of immovability. In touching the earth he calls to witness the previous compassionate actions performed in his lives on earth which provided the strength (i.e., his store of merit) to resist his own desire for life.

As night began, he ascended the eight stages of concentration known as the "eight dhyāna(s)," which he had mastered under his teachers, and during the four divisions of the night achieved a deepening understanding of the nature of existence, which understanding constituted his enlightenment. It is the content of his enlightenment experience which formed both the basis of his teaching and his authority to teach. It may be said that the entire subsequent history of the Buddhadharma is simply a progressive explanation, systematization and interpretation of this experience.

In the first watch of the night Shākyamuni saw all of his previous lives. As the text says, he saw that in such and such a place he had such and such a name and lived a certain life history. That is, he directly perceived all his previous lives, almost as if reviewing a motion picture series of biographies in total detail.

In the second watch of the night he obtained the divine wisdom eye and saw the whole universe of birth and death as if in a mirror. That is, he directly perceived, with the clarity and passivity of a mirror, the death and rebirth of all beings. Particularly importantly, he saw that of the five realms into which beings could be reborn, the realm into which they were in fact reborn was the result of their own actions: their rebirths were determined by their own karma, a word which literally means "action."

In the third watch of the night he obtained the extinction of the outflows and perceived the more detailed operation of karma. The text says that he perceived the four truths and the twelve limbs of dependent origination, which formulations are the detailed working out of the law of karma and the truth of selflessness.

Finally, in the fourth watch of the night he obtained omniscience, and when the sun rose, he was Shākyamuni no longer, but a Buddha, "an enlightened one," "an awakened one."

We may interpret this enlightenment experience as a progressive unfoldment of a single truth about existence, whose implications are amplified over the course of the night. When the whole of this truth and all of its implications are not just comprehended, but directly perceived, the goal of the religious quest has been obtained. What is this one truth? Most simply put, it is causality and all its implications, but certainly not causality as we understand it.

The causality that the Buddha speaks of is "dependent origination" (Sanskrit: pratītyasamutpāda, Tibetan: brten 'brel). Formally, this causality is described by the following standard formulation:

> When this is present, that comes to be; from the arising of this, that arises. When this is absent, that does not come to be, on the cessation of this, that ceases.[1]

This is not causality in the sense of some mechanistic physics of western science where the action of one object powers the action of some other object, much like one billiard ball striking another billiard ball and setting it in motion. Something else is being described by the Buddha which can be best understood through the use of an example derived from his enlightenment experience.

As we saw, in the third watch of the night Shākyamuni directly perceived the "twelve limbs of dependent origination." According to some current scholarly interpretations, this twelve limb formulation is a later compilation[2] and in some of the oldest texts recording the Buddha's dialogues the full twelvefold formulation is not to be found, although its elements are indeed embedded in the oldest texts. The Buddha usually speaks about several of the limbs in combination, and in one location, in a later text, speaks of eight of the limbs. Scholars do agree, however, that even if the full twelve limb formulation is a later scholastic elaboration, and in this form cannot be directly attributed to the Buddha, still it does represent a compilation of something essential in his teaching and enlightenment experience.

TWELVE LIMBS OF DEPENDENT ORIGINATION

1.	Ignorance	ma rig pa
2.	Karmic formations	'du byed
3.	Consciousness	rnam par shes pa
4.	Name and form	ming dang gzugs
5.	Six sense fields	skye mched drug
6.	Contact	reg pa
7.	Feelings	tshor ba
8.	Craving	sred pa
9.	Grasping	nye bar len pa
10.	Becoming	srid pa
11.	Birth	skye ba
12.	Death, grief, suffering	rga 'i

These twelve limbs represent various aspects of the human being in conjunction with his/her environment, and can only be understood when viewed as an interconnected complex, which is why they are often portrayed on the rim of a wheel: the circular rim symbolizing the beginningless interconnectedness of these twelve features. They cannot be properly understood if viewed as separate disconnected entities, though they are elaborated separately and identified as "first limb" or "seventh limb," etc. The limbs designate features of a complete field, but the field and its features only have real meaning when viewed as a dynamic whole. It is taught that these twelve limbs arise in dependence on each other, and it is certainly this arising or origination in dependence that Shākyamuni saw on the night of his enlightenment.

Let us begin our description with the fourth through seventh limbs. The fourth limb is identified as "name and form" (ming dang gzugs), which is a Buddhist technical term for the psychophysical entity usually called a person. "Name" identifies consciousness and its various aspects while "form" identifies matter and its various aspects. Included under "name" are the aggregates (skandha, phung po) of feeling, perception, karmic formations and consciousness; that is, all the immaterial aspects of a being[3] (more on this shortly). The fifth limb is identified as "the six sense fields" or "gateways" or "entrances" (skye mched drug) that is, the six fields in which consciousness operates. These are the fields of the eye, ear, nose, tongue, body (i.e., tactile senses) and mind. It may seem odd to list mind as a sense organ; this will be explained under section 1-3 below. Suffice it to say for the moment that mind is considered an organ whose objects are concepts, mental images and other sense consciousnesses; for example, the concept "me" or the image of a person who is identified as "me." The sixth limb is identified as "contact" (reg pa), that is, the coming together of an object of perception, a sense organ and a consciousness; for example, an eye, a material form and a visual consciousness. The seventh limb is identified as "feelings" (tshor ba), which are either pleasant, painful, or neither pleasant nor painful. There are six classes of feelings, in accordance with the sense organ upon which the feeling depends.

"Depend" is the key word here, for what is described in the twelve limbs scheme is not a causal chain in the strict sense of causality as understood by modern western science. It would, for example, be incorrect to say that name and form cause the six sense fields in the way that the kinetic energy of one billiard ball causes the movement of a second billiard ball which it strikes. Rather, the existence of matter is a prerequisite for the existence of a sense organ, such as an eye, which is a prerequisite for the existence of a visual field. Likewise, the occurrence of contact between an eye, a material form and a visual consciousness is a prerequisite for the occurrence of a feeling of pleasure in regards to a pleasing sight. Thus it is said that the phenomenon of feeling arises in dependence on the phenomenon of contact, that the phenomenon of contact arises in dependence on the phenomenon of a sense field, and that the phenomenon of a sense field arises in dependence on the phenomenon of name and form, the psychophysical being.

The Buddha, after all, is teaching about his experience, he is teaching a phenomenology. Thus he posits the observed connections between phenomena; he is not speaking about forces which effect things in some mechanistic physics. Dependent origination, however, does not necessarily thereby exclude this sort of strict causality. It could be argued that contact does indeed "cause" feeling, although the Buddha does not formulate his teaching in this way because in other cases one limb does not "cause" a second limb. For example, the eye does not "cause" contact; rather its existence is required before there can be visual contact. Thus, causality, as understood by modern western science, could be considered a special case of the larger category of relations designated by the term "dependent origination."

Proceeding then on through the twelve limbs: "craving" (sred pa) arises in dependence on "contact," and "grasping" (nye bar len pa) arises in dependence on "craving."

That is, we crave pleasant sense experiences and grasp after their continuation, while we crave the cessation of painful sense experiences and grasp after their cessation. It was the Buddha's experience in the course of his enlightenment that all phenomena arise and cease, and so, of course, feelings must arise and cease. But we crave for the pleasant to remain and grasp after it even though it may begin to cease, and we crave for the unpleasant to cease and grasp after it, even though it may remain for longer than we wish. This cycle of grasping after the transitory is the nature of our existence; it is the limb of "becoming" (srid pa) and it depends upon craving for sense objects and the pleasures or pains associated with them, especially the grasping after objects and feelings appropriated to the notion "I," a concept which is the object of the sense organ known as "mind" (yid).

It was the Buddha's experience that our becoming does not begin with this particular life, nor does it end with it. On the night of his enlightenment he saw his own beginningless series of lives, and the continuua of lives of others. This continuum of life depends upon our firmly grasping after the continued existence of "I" with its associated sense experiences so that upon the cessation of one particular life we obtain another. And of course whatever is born will die; thus birth occurs in dependence on becoming and in dependence on birth is death.

Now the notion that grasping after the continued existence of a self, i.e., the experience of "I-ness," could bring about a new birth is particularly foreign to the Judeo-Christian mind. To understand this aspect of the twelve limbs it is best to work our way around backwards from the fourth limb, "name and form," to the first, "ignorance" (ma rig pa), and then to the twelfth, "death, grief, suffering" (rga 'i) and the eleventh, "birth" (skye ba). For the twelve limbs are a closed circle in which every limb depends upon the previous eleven. So ignorance depends on death, just as death depends upon ignorance.

Buddha taught that "name and form" originate in de-

pendence on the third limb, "consciousness" (rnam par
shes pa). From one perspective, no body ("form") could
exist without consciousness, for then it would be dead.
Sleep is not considered an exception here, for sleep is considered to be a total unawareness of objects of sense, i.e.,
consciousness of nothing, not a nonexistence of consciousness; thus it is said that the continuity of consciousness
persists even during dreamless sleep.[4] From another perspective, for the ordinary person consciousness is never experienced devoid of the influences of previous experience.
These previous experiences leave traces in memory which
mold consciousness (more on this in section 1-4). Thus
consciousness depends on the second limb, "dispositions"
or "karmic formations" (saṁskāra, 'du byed). Here the
term "formations" is important, for the traces left by previous actions (karma, las) form the consciousness in certain
ways: it is never "raw consciousness" uninfluenced by past
actions.

The karmic formations themselves arise in dependence
on the first limb, "ignorance." Here ignorance means an
unknowing of the real nature or existential status of phenomena, both internal and external. Rather, because of
previous experience humans interpret things and react to
them in the context of desires and aversions, thus overesti-
mating the attractive and repulsive aspects of phenomena.
People do not see things for what they are, but rather see
them in a distorted fashion. This distorted perception and
conception is habitual, thus the "consciousness" which
arises in dependence on "karmic formations" is fundamentally distorted by "ignorance."

This ignorance is so deep that it could not depend on the
experiences of a single life but rather depends on the experiences of a multiplicity of lives; thus it depends on the
previous limbs (eleven and twelve) of "birth" and "death."
Moreover, it is especially the pleasures and sufferings of
lives which leave the traces which distort consciousness: it
is the shrinking from the unpleasant and the grasping after
the pleasant, the pain of birth and the terror of death, the

frustration of growing old and feeble that leave the most profound traces on consciousness. It is the inability to experience these things just as they are, without blocking or warping our experiences of them, that leave distorted traces (klesha, nyon mongs pa) on consciousness. Even the pleasant things in life are grasped after with an unwarranted desire which overestimates the pleasure they will give, and is accompanied by a constant fear of their loss.

Thus we can see that the twelve limbs of dependent origination describe the course of the unfolding existence of beings in a dynamic way. Life after life, as the Buddha saw on the night of his enlightenment, beings grasp after transitory satisfactions in an ignorant fashion. It is "grasping" that impels beings into the flux of rebirth, but this grasping itself ultimately depends upon "ignorance," which is an incorrect understanding of the actual nature of phenomena and the consequent attraction to or revulsion from these phenomena. Thus, the twelve limbs are often described as a wheel, with the limbs themselves comprising the rim and the "three poisons" of delusion (gti mug), attraction or lust ('dod chags) and revulsion or hatred (zhe sdang) forming the hub of the wheel. The Buddha saw beings as endlessly cycling through this existence whose nature is described by the twelve limbs, moment by moment turning on the hub of the three poisons. This is the state of things, which he called "saṁsāra" ('khor ba).

But the Buddha also saw that there was a way out of this cycle, a way to "get off the wheel," or stop its turning. Because each of the twelve limbs is a condition upon which the others depend, if any of these conditions could be destroyed, the entire cycle would cease. This cessation of the cycle is what he called "nirvāṇa" (mya ngan las 'das pa), and it can come about precisely because each of the twelve conditions arises in dependence upon the others: if one limb were to cease, so the whole interdependent chain would break.

The Buddha expressed this formally as the "Four Noble Truths," which was his perception on the night of his enlightenment that because the unpleasantness (sdug bsngal) of existence (the first truth) depends upon ignorant grasping (the second truth), so upon the cessation of this ignorant grasping, the unpleasantness would also cease (the third truth). This cessation is, again, referred to as "nir-vāṇa," a term which literally means "blowing out," i.e., the blowing out or cooling of the passions, the ignorant grasping after satisfaction. He also saw how to bring this cessation about, which is, formally, the Buddhist path (the fourth truth), that is, what one can do to break the chain of the twelve limbs of dependent origination.

If we consider this formulation of the twelve limbs we will note that although it is a dynamic description of the relations between motivation, habits, actions and consequences, nowhere does it make mention of a person to whom these consequences occur, although the occurrence of consequences for actions is certain (as the Buddha saw in the second watch of the night). This is quite intentional, for in the third watch of the night the Buddha not only perceived the operation of the twelve limbs and the Four Noble Truths, but also the truth of selflessness (bdag min). What does this selflessness mean?

It is best to answer this question by looking for the closest thing to a "person" in the twelve limbs which the Buddha perceived in the third watch of the night (in which he also perceived the truth of selflessness). The closest thing to a person in the twelve limbs is "name and form" (the fourth limb). Form means matter, which is composed of the "four great elements" ('byung ba chen po bzhi): earth, air, fire and water. When we perceive something, it is this form which, at base, we are actually perceiving. It is also the basis for the human body, the compound of various organs, bones, etc. which is the physical basis of a "person." "Name" is the consciousness which does the perceiving of forms: it is what is commonly referred to as "mind." Like the body, it is not a unity, but rather a compound of various factors which are generally grouped into four classes. These

four are: feelings, of which there are either pleasant, painful, or neither pleasant nor painful feelings; perceptions, of
which there are six, in accordance with their sense organ
basis; karmic formations, of which there are many classes
which are meant to include all the traces of previous experience plus some basic characteristics of the functioning of
attention and memory; and raw consciousness itself, pure
awareness unmolded by the karmic formations or perceptions, which are other classes. One will immediately note
that these classes (which are called "aggregates:" skan-
dha(s), phung po) include four of the other eleven limbs,
although the perception skandha differs slightly from the
limb of the six sense fields, as the limb designates the
organs of perception while the skandha refers to the perceiving of objects, and the consciousness skandha differs
from the consciousness limb as it is consciousness considered in the abstract, without the molding effect of the
karmic formations.

What we have here are two intersecting descriptive systems. The skandha system is static and analytic; it describes
the components, as it were, which make up a person. The
twelve limbs system is dynamic: it describes the way the
skandha(s) interact in the course of the unfoldment of human existence and how they effect each other over time.

Nowhere in the skandha description do we find reference
to a person. One could identify a subjective thought "I"
within this system as a memory or name, in which case it
would fall into the karmic formations skandha. Or one
could identify that thought "I" as an object of perception of
the mind sense, in which case it would fall into the perception skandha. But nowhere would there be found an organ
or entity, as it were, which was an actual "I" or "ego." It is
this self which is nowhere to be found as an actual entity,
but is to be found merely as a label applied to subjective
experiences, which is identified by the Buddha in his
teaching of the selflessness of the person. What the Buddha
saw in the third watch of the night was that the being which

we take to be a person was simply the five skandha(s) arising and ceasing over many continued existences. Nowhere was an actual person or self to be identified; thus beings are empty of a self, or "selfless."

Now, the Buddha did not say that there was no subjective "I," but rather that there was no *actual person* to act as a referent for the concept "I." It is clear that we all use the label "I" and all experience an "I" as an apparent subject of "our" experiences, but the Buddha showed that upon analysis no actual entity of a self can be found that corresponds to that experience of "I" which is wrapped up in common subjective experience. If there were an actual self or person or being that corresponded to the subjective sense of "I," then it should be findable upon analysis of the human being. As all of a human being can be found within the sort system of the five skandha(s), so an actual self should be found there also. Yet, if the form skandha is removed, is a self to be found? Or if the consciousness skandha is removed, is a self to be found? No matter where one looks within the five skandha(s) no actual self is to be found, only an idea of an "I" which is supposed to be a self or refer to a self. Moreover, nothing associated with a human being can be found outside of the five skandha(s). Thus, the Buddha taught that the idea of a self arises in dependence upon the five skandha(s) and ceases when they cease, but if they were to be separated, no actual self could be found either within one of them or as a remainder left over after the process of separation. Thus, no self actually exists, there is merely a label "I" which refers to a nonexistent self and which is imputed upon or designated upon the five skandha(s).

It is the essence of ignorance to believe that such a self exists at the core of beings and to grasp after such a self; indeed that is why beings are reborn. Moreover, the belief that there is an actual self which can be designated by the label "self" or "I" or the experience "me" is only a special case of the general ignorant habit of believing that there are actual entities of any kind which are the objects of reference for any labels and which bear the characteristics attributed to them by the labels. It is the demonstration of this subtle selflessness of entities or phenomena which is Nāgārjuna's basic discourse in his *Seventy Stanzas* (cf. section 1-6).

It is also the destruction of this ignorant and distorted belief that selves and things are what they appear to be that breaks the chain of the twelve limbs, that brings about the nirvāṇa which the Buddha proclaimed. For, as ultimately all the limbs arise in dependence on ignorance, and ignorance is primarily the belief in self where there is no actual self, so upon the cessation of this incorrect belief, the whole complex of the twelve limbs breaks down, the five skandha(s) have no basis for coming together, rebirth stops, and suffering ceases.

But if there is no actual person, what is reborn in the first place, and what is freed in nirvāṇa? The Buddha's experience in the second watch of his night of enlightenment certified that actions bear fruit in future lives, and that beings would be reborn in one of five realms. How does this connect with his experience in the third watch of the night, that beings lack selfhood? The answer is that the skandha of consciousness is a continuum of moments of consciousness, and although this continuum is constantly changing as perception changes and as the various karmic formations mold consciousness, the continuum itself is without beginning or end. Thus the taking of rebirth is simply the connection of a new body with the continuum of changing moments of consciousness which preexisted in connection with an old body. And with the connection to a new body the idea of "I" arises again, and the experiences of the new body are appropriated to that "I" which is, in fact, without an actual self as a referent, but merely appears to the continuum of moments of consciousness the way any other idea or object would appear.

Section 1-3 Perception and Conception

It should be apparent from the preceeding section that the Buddha's teaching about the path to salvation is highly psychological. That beings are bound to a suffering existence is primarily a result of ignorance; that they can become free is primarily a result of dispelling ignorance through acquiring its opposite, wisdom. As the Buddha's own personal path included mental disciplines, an analysis of the mind's operation, and the acquiring of merit through compassionate activity, one should not be surprised that the universal path which he then taught also relied heavily upon an analysis of the mind.

Let us begin this analysis of the mind from an epistemological perspective (that of Dharmakīrti),[1] and ask, what is involved in perception? By doing so, we can begin in the same place where we began our analysis of the twelve limbs of dependent origination, with the fourth limb (name and form, ming dang gzugs) and the fifth limb (six sense fields, skye mched drug). Perception, recall, is described as both a skandha and as one of the twelve limbs: the limb of the six sense fields. From the point of view of the basic psychophysical organism (name and form) which does the perceiving and is the basis for the designation "person," the perception skandha and the six sense fields limb can be combined, as in the following chart, which organizes the basic psychophysical perceptual situation.

OBJECTIVE FIELD	SENSE ORGAN	CONSCIOUSNESS
forms	eye	visual consciousness
gzugs	mig	mig gi rnams par shes pa
sounds	ear	auditory consciousness
sgra	rna	rna ba'i rnams par shes pa
smells	nose	olfactory consciousness
dri	sna	sna'i rnams par shes pa
tastes	tongue	gustatory consciousness
ro	lce	lce'i rnams par shes pa
tangibles	body	tactile consciousness
reg bya	lus	lus kyi rnams par shes pa
concepts	mind	mental consciousness
chos	yid	yid kyi rnams par shes pa

This chart indicates the limits of human cognition: all cognitions are limited by our senses, of which there are six. There are five types of material sense cognition and one type of nonmaterial mental sense cognition, i.e., mental consciousness. Actual perception occurs when there is contact (the sixth limb) between a sense organ, an object in its field and consciousness. For example, seeing is the contact between a form, the eye and consciousness. It is said that these three arise and cease together over a sequence of moments. A moment (skad chig) is a very short duration of time: it is said that there are sixty five of these moments in the time it takes to snap a finger, so a moment is defined as a period of time equivalent to one sixty fifth of a finger snap.

It should be noted that although the chart above seems to identify six different types of consciousness, there is actually only one fundamental consciousness (consciousness skandha, rnam shes, or consciousness limb, usually designated "primary consciousness," sems, or "consciousness," shes pa). But as consciousness always arises and ceases moment by moment in conjunction with a sense organ, and is modified or molded by habits and attentional factors (usually designated "secondary mental factors," sems 'byung, cf. section 1-4), it is always experienced as a certain "type" of consciousness. That is, consciousness (defined as an awareness which is clear and knowing, gsal zhing rig pa) is always consciousness of something.

What this chart signifies for the first five (material) senses is clear, but what it signifies for the sixth sense, mind, is less clear. Here mind does not mean brain, or even some nonmaterial cognitive organ, but something different. Recall that consciousness is said to arise and cease as a series of moments, and that any phenomenon which arises does so in dependence on certain causes and conditions or prerequisites; this is the dependent origination discussed in section 1-2. Visual consciousness, for example, arises in dependence on three conditions: a dominant condition (dbag rkyen), the eye organ, which makes it a "visual" consciousness; an object condition (dmigs rkyen), a form, which is the sort of object taken by an eye; and an immediate condition (de ma thag rkyen), the actual cause, which is the immediately preceeding moment of consciousness. These three conditions are required for a moment of visual consciousness to arise. The immediate condition, which is the immediately preceeding moment of consciousness, is a requirement because consciousness does not occur in a vacuum; each moment of consciousness is simply and necessarily part of a stream of moments of consciousness stretching into the past and future. Consciousness has a continuity, a continuum. In the chart above, what is called "mind" (yid), which is the "organ" or dominant condition upon which mental consciousness depends is simply the preceeding moment of consciousness. Thus mind(organ) is both a dominant condition and an immediate condition for mental consciousness. It is in this way that mind(organ) is immaterial and is not a thing or "organ" proper, as is an eye.

What constitutes the object condition for the arising of a moment of mental consciousness? Whereas the first five (material sense) consciousnesses in our chart are primarily receptive, passively receiving impressions of material objects, the sixth consciousness, mental consciousness, is responsive and reflective. The five material sense consciousnesses apprehend their objects through the force of the objects appearing to them. The sixth, mental, consciousness apprehends its objects primarily due to the influence of subjective dispositions, the secondary mental factors. The objects of mental consciousness could be concepts, memories, emotional states, or perceptions, i.e., one or more of the five material sense consciousnesses. In the case of perceptions being the objects of mental consciousness, we need to understand that a perception is actually just a moment of a perceptual consciousness and is the moment of consciousness immediately preceeding the arising of a moment of conceptual, mental consciousness taking that perception as its object. Thus, for a mental consciousness whose object is a perception, such as a visual consciousness, the dominant condition, the object condition and the immediate condition are the same: the immediately preceeding moment of a consciousness, such as a visual consciousness.

Generally speaking, the five material sense perceptions and mental perception work together, arising and ceasing moment by moment, and so creating our image of the world. However, we tend not to be aware of the "raw image" created in perceptual consciousness because mental consciousness also registers concepts, memories and emotions from the side of the observer, and these enter into the representation of the total perceptual field which constitutes our cognitions. To understand how this process works it is necessary to look in greater detail at the three conditions upon which a mental consciousness depends.

When there is contact between, say, a form, an eye and a visual consciousness, a visual perception occurs. It lasts for just one moment, although it can recur as a series of subsequent moments. That first fresh moment of a bare visual consciousness would be a cognition of a mere form of a certain color. However, that first fresh moment of a bare visual consciousness can serve as the condition for the arising of a moment of mental consciousness, in which case one would, in that second moment, have a mental perception of a visual consciousness. But due to the power of the subjective secondary mental factors (derived from past memories, emotions and concepts, i.e., the karmic formations skandha), a memory or mental image (don spyi) will arise at that same moment as the arising of the mental consciousness and will, for all subsequent moments of the arising of the visual consciousness associated with a specific object, be mixed with that visual consciousness and these together will serve as the condition for the arising of all subsequent moments of mental consciousness. Thus, except for the initial moment of the arising of a visual consciousness of a certain object, all the subsequent moments of that visual consciousness which serve as an object for a mental consciousness will be mixed with mental images, memories, emotional responses, etc., and these will serve as the condition for the arising of mental consciousness. During those subsequent moments the mental consciousness will not be able to perceive the visual consciousness free of the mental images and subjective dispositions mixed with it. Thus, ordinary mental consciousness cannot directly perceive the material sense consciousnesses or their appearing objects (snang yul).

This point is most important, for in the initial moment of a cognition of a certain object the five material sense consciousnesses do directly perceive their objects nonerroneously because these perceptual consciousnesses are not mixed with a mental image. However, during the subsequent moments of the arising of these sense consciousnesses which are cognizing a certain object they are mixed with mental images and this whole complex serves as object condition, dominant condition and immediately preceeding condition for the arising of mental consciousness. Such a mental consciousness, which is what we commonly refer to as "thought," or our "thinking mind," is therefore unable to separate the mental images from the actual bare perceptions, and is thus *always* erroneous and distorted in that it confuses this mixture of mental image and perceptual consciousness for the object itself. This mental consciousness which takes such a mixture of mental images and perceptual consciousnesses as an object is called a conceptual type of cognition, while a bare perceptual consciousness which is unmixed with any mental images is called a perceptual type of cognition.

Since the whole point of the Buddha's teaching was to show how beings are bound to suffering existence through ignorant grasping, and since ignorance is defined as erroneous understanding of the nature of phenomena, so the analysis of how conceptual cognition is fundamentally erroneous becomes the essential issue in determining how to develop nonerroneous, i.e., valid cognitions (tshad ma). Note, again, that perceptual cognitions in and of themselves are generally valid, but that a person only has them for moments of such brevity that they are generally not observed before they are mixed with mental images.

What one generally does observe as the stream of moments of consciousness are conceptual cognitions which take perceptions as objects, for these persist for many moments subsequent to the perceptual cognition, and so far and away occupy most of a person's attention.

The problem with conceptual cognition, as we have seen, is the mixing of the mental images with perceptions; this is what produces erroneous conceptual cognition; this, along with the erroneous innate belief in selfhood or entityness of phenomena, is the source of ignorance, the first of the twelve limbs. If this erroneous view could be corrected and this process could be suspended, then there would be no ignorance (the first limb) to serve as the condition for the arising of the karmic formations (the second limb), which distort consciousness (the third limb), and so forth. Thus the whole twelve limb complex would be dismembered and nirvāṇa would be obtained.

These mental images (don spyi) are not necessarily subjective visual replications of an external object, although they could be. Rather, a mental image is usually a complex of images, ideas, assumptions, beliefs and emotions which are interconnected in a single image-like pattern. For example, a person may have never been to Lhasa, but has read about this city and may have a variety of vague images of what it might be like. He or she might even know something about the history of the city and the events which have taken place there, and these too are connected to the mental image of Lhasa. Moreover, a person may, having read about Lhasa, have a strong desire to go there. This whole complex of information about Lhasa, a place that this person has never visited, forms his or her mental image of Lhasa. Whenever he or she hears the word "Lhasa" this image of Lhasa is, after the first moment of auditory consciousness, immediately mixed with all subsequent moments of auditory consciousness as well as all the subsequent moments of mental conceptual consciousness which depend upon that initial nonconceptual moment of auditory consciousness. This type of mental image is called a nominal mental image (sgra spyi), as it is based upon words. If, however, a person were to visit Lhasa, and then after leaving the city someone were to ask about Lhasa, the person would have a mental image of Lhasa based upon their experience of it. This would be an experiential mental image (don spyi). Of course these two can be mixed, as when a person reads about Lhasa and then visits Lhasa. In a general sense, we refer to such mental images as conceptions (rtog pa), because especially in the case of nominal mental images, the conception is not an exact replication of the object which is its referent, but strictly speaking, conceptions are based upon mental images.

Conceptual cognitions can be distinguished in two ways, depending on whether they simply give a name to an object or ascribe certain qualities to an object. For example, upon seeing a picture of Lhasa, one might think, "That is Lhasa;" this is called a term-connecting conception (ming sbyar ba'i rtog pa), because the conceptual consciousness has apprehended its object through the use of the term "Lhasa." However, if upon seeing the picture of Lhasa one were to think "That place is very large," that would be a fact-connecting conception (don sbyar ba'i rtog pa), because the conceptual consciousness has apprehended its object through ascribing certain characteristics to it. These two types of conception may also be mixed.

Dharmakīrti's epistemology teaches that all conceptual cognitions are deceived in regards to their objects because they apprehend their objects through the medium of a conception, i.e., either a nominal mental image or an experiential mental image or a fact-connecting conception or a term-connecting conception, or some combination of them. This deception is necessarily the case because in the first moment of a conceptual cognition (which is also the second moment of a perceptual cognition) the mixing of the conception and the perceptual consciousness will begin and will continue for all subsequent moments of that cognition. Because the mental consciousness of the conceptual cognition cannot separate the conception from the perception it is said to be deceived about the mode of appearance of the object as well as the mode of existence of the object. The mode of appearance of the object refers to how the object appears in consciousness (that is, the mode of appearance is the mixture of the mental image with the bare perception); the mode of existence of the object refers to how the object actually exists in and of itself. For example, if one cognizes a red rose growing on a vine before one, one's cognition of the rose is said to be deceived because one is incapable of separating one's conceptions about the rose from the mere appearance of a red shape, which is all that is actually cognized by a visual consciousness. Moreover as one neither thinks, "This rose is impermanent," nor perceives the impermanence of the rose, but rather just sees a rose as if it were permanently there, so one is deceived about the mode of existence of the rose, which is, after all, impermanent. If, however, when one cognizes a red rose one were to think, "This rose is impermanent," then one would not be deceived about the mode of existence of the rose, but would still be deceived about the mode of appearance of the rose, for one would still be mixing the red shape with the conception "rose," thus cognizing a rose which was impermanent.

The examples given above have all been of cognitions oriented toward experiences of the present, but one can also recollect past objects or experiences and imagine future objects and experiences. Such cognitions are similar to cognitions of present objects and experiences except that they are not mixed with perceptual cognitions.

It is important to understand the way these conceptual cognitions develop because according to Buddhist teachings erroneous, distorted cognitions are the source of all our troubles, they are the reason why our activities in the world produce suffering rather than peace. However, it is possible to develop cognitions which are not erroneous and deceived; such cognitions lead to actions which bring about peace rather than suffering. Just as there are erroneous perceptual cognitions and erroneous conceptual cognitions, so there are nonerroneous and valid perceptual cognitions (mngon sum tshad ma) and nonerroneous and valid conceptual cognitions (rjes dpag tshad ma). These are referred to as ideal or perfect or valid cognitions or states of consciousness. Different schools of Buddhist thought have differing opinions about these perfect cognitions. In the Sautrāntika system, for example, only the first moment of perceptual cognition of an object can be a perfect cognition, all subsequent moments in the stream of moments of that particular

cognition are not considered perfect because they are induced by the force of that first moment. However, in this
book we are following the Prāsaṅgika Mādhyamika view,
and from this perspective both the first moment of cognition and all the subsequent moments of cognition which
arise in dependence on that first moment may be perfect
cognitions if they have certain characteristics, which are
described below. On the other hand, since phenomena are
actually impermanent and change from moment to moment, it can be argued that each moment of perceptual
cognition of a particular object is the first moment of perceptual cognition of that particular object, because the object has changed over the course of moments, and is a
different object each moment. Thus in this regard, there is
not so much difference between the view of the Sautrāntikas and the Prāsaṅgikas.

What then is a perfect, and therefore valid, cognition?
According to the Sautrāntikas it must be fresh and infallible
(mi slu ba). Fresh means that it is the first moment of
cognition of an object in a series of moments which cognize
a particular object. According to the Prāsaṅgikas this is not
a requirement, as all subsequent moments of the cognitive
series can be interpreted as initial moments, as indicated
above. The second aspect of a perfect cognition is its infalli-
bility. This means that a perfect cognition correctly ascertains its object and eliminates misconceptions about it. Both
perceptual cognitions and conceptual cognitions can be
valid, perfect cognitions, although a perceptual cognition
must be nonconceptual to be valid while a conceptual cognition must be established on the basis of a perfect reason or
inference (rjes dpag) to be valid. Two examples will help. A
perception of a rose which creates a sufficient impression on
consciousness to induce a cognition that ascertains its object
is a valid perception. Thus the mere seeing of the rose is a
valid perception. A conception which is based on valid
reasoning, such as "sound is impermanent" is a valid conceptual cognition, because impermanence is the mode of

existence of sound. In both these examples, the perceptual cognition of the rose and the conceptual cognition of the impermanence of sound, the cognitions are infallible because they induce certainty about their objects: one is certain of what is seen or one is certain that all sounds are impermanent because on the basis of valid reasoning one had ascertained that all sounds must eventually cease.

This is a very important point, because if it were not possible to have valid perceptual cognitions it would not be possible to correctly perceive the world, and if it were not possible to have valid conceptual cognitions, it would not be possible to eradicate ignorance, i.e., replace erroneous conceptions with valid conceptions.

One might think that all perceptual cognitions are infallible, because they all induce certainty about their objects, but this is not so. Many perceptions are, for example, inattentive. Indeed, for ordinary persons, the first moment of perceptual cognition is always inattentive, which is why ordinary persons don't see things for what they are, devoid of mixing them with mental images. Inattentive perception (snang la ma nges pa) means that a perception is not attended to because it is either so brief that it does not register in the observing consciousness, as in the case above, or else that the observing consciousness is so intent on some object that it does not register other perceptions. A case here might be that of a person driving a car and being so attentive to the traffic that he or she did not notice the clouds on the horizon, even though those clouds were in their field of perception. Such inattentive perception of the clouds could not induce certainty about them, for if you asked the driver if the clouds were white or grey, he or she couldn't answer.

Similarly, there are mistaken sensory perceptions (rtog med log shes su 'gyur pa'i dbang shes), such as mirages, the seeing of the world as yellow because one suffers from jaundice, and so forth. These perceptual cognitions are invalid not because they are incapable of inducing certainty about their objects, but because they are deceived about their objects due to a defect in the sense organ or due to certain factors in the overall perceptual situation.

Just as there are mistaken sensory cognitions, so there are mistaken conceptual cognitions (rtog pa log shes). It is obvious that the belief that the earth is flat, or that rabbits have horns is mistaken. The real problem lies with mistaken conceptions about subtle aspects of phenomena. For example, the conception that sound is impermanent will probably become obvious to anyone that thinks about it, and the conception that a rose is impermanent, though one probably does not think about this upon initially perceiving a rose, will also become obvious should one think about it. However, it is harder to think about our own impermanence and arrive at certainty about that, for we naturally think of ourselves as permanent. Such a cognition of permanence about oneself is simply a mistaken cognition; however, one can reason about the situation and develop a correct belief (yid dpyod) that one is indeed impermanent. Such a correct belief is not, however, a valid cognition, for it will not induce certainty about this impermanence of oneself.

In the case given above, the syllogism which underlies the development of the correct belief would be as follows: All persons are impermanent; I am a person; therefore, I am impermanent. This syllogism is correct, but the referent, an actually existent person, has no actual existential status or basis. This is because the person or self which is the object of the conception of impermanence can never be found, for it does not actually exist as an object, but rather simply exists as a name or designation. The preceeding syllogism is, in essence, no different than the following: All persons are impermanent; the son of a barren woman is a person; therefore, the son of a barren woman is impermanent. The problem, of course, is that there is no actual existential referent for "the son of a barren woman," so permanence or impermanence is out of the question. On the other hand, the statement that "I am impermanent because

'I' is a mere designation upon the transitory skandha(s)"
goes beyond being a correct belief, and is a valid conceptual
cognition of its referent "I." This is because in this case the
cognition has grasped the true existential status of its referent, and so can induce certainty about it.

The whole point of Nāgārjuna's discourse in the *Seventy
Stanzas* is to convert mistaken conceptions into correct
beliefs and, eventually, valid cognitions. This can be done
through the use of a logical exposition and is the method
referred to as "prasaṅga," (which is the root for the name
applied to Candrakīrti's school, Prāsaṅgika Mādhyamika.
It is the school of thought followed by the Tibetans upon
whose expositions this book is based). However, developing
a correct belief is not adequate for obtaining liberation, it is
only a preliminary. Yet this preliminary is important, because based upon correct beliefs one can move on to develop valid cognitions. As said above, one aspect of a valid
cognition is its ability to induce certainty about its referent;
a correct belief can contribute to the development of such a
valid conceptual cognition. Yet even this is not enough for
liberation, for the problem with valid conceptual cognitions
is that they are conceptual, that is, they ascertain their
objects through the use of a mental image or conception,
and even valid conceptual cognitions cannot separate the
mental image or conception from the bare perception mixed
with it so as to directly and nonconceptually cognize the
object (mngon sum tshad ma), which is what is required to
break the saṁsāric twelve limb cycle. An Ārya, however,
can directly and nonconceptually cognize objects.

As was said above, conceptual cognitions always confuse
the appearing object (snang yul) with the referent object of
bare nonconceptual perceptual cognition. Thus even if one
were to have a correct belief or valid conceptual cognition,
such as "sound is impermanent," nevertheless, cognizing
the conception "sound is impermanent" is not the same as
directly cognizing impermanence, as an Ārya would. On
the other hand, unless one first correctly reasons that sound

is impermanent, one will not be able to go on to directly and nonconceptually cognize impermanence. In a manner of speaking, a correct belief or valid conceptual cognition shows one where to look, but then must be removed or else it will obscure the view. This is perhaps more obvious if one utilizes a subtle example, such as the lack of actual selfhood for persons. First one must reason about what selflessness means, and come to understand how the conception of a self or a person is something which is merely imputed or super-imposed (sgro 'dogs) upon the five skandha(s). Having developed a correct belief about this lack of selfhood in the apparent person does not mean that one will be absolutely certain about it, for one will continue to act as if one were really a self identified by a certain name. One must utilize the correct belief about selflessness, which is a mental im-age, a conception, to develop a valid conceptual cognition and use this as a theme for meditation. Thus practicing, one can eventually come to see the actual mixing of the concep-tion of selflessness with the perception of a specific being. However, this is still a mixture of a mental image with a perception, and is not a direct nonconceptual perception itself. Yet, if one continues to practice, one can then remove the mental image, and one will be left with a bare direct perceptual cognition of a being which lacks selfhood. Upon obtaining such a direct cognition one is said to have become an Ārya and have obtained the Path of Seeing.[2]

The cognition of the lacking of selfhood in a being was initially induced by the valid conceptual cognition, which showed one where to direct one's attention when meditat-ing, but once one can directly and nonconceptually cognize the lack of selfhood in a being, then that direct, fresh, nonconceptual cognition will induce certainty about the lack of selfhood in beings: one will *experience* this lack of selfhood in beings. This is a valid perceptual cognition, and will remove the misunderstandings about selfhood which have accumulated over the cycle of countless lives. Because such valid cognitions destroy ignorance, they are liberative;

they break the cycle of the twelve limbs which is saṁsāra.

To summarize, there are two key operations in the practical application of Dharmakīrti's epistemology: developing valid conceptual cognitions and separating mental images from perceptions. Nāgārjuna's discourse in the *Seventy Stanzas* establishes the valid cognitions about both persons and phenomena (things, for example). One of the most important points he establishes is that the objects of perception are different from our conceptions or mental images of them. Thus, Nāgārjuna devotes considerable attention to showing that what we take for objects of perception which have certain qualities or characteristics inherent in them are actually pervaded by deluded conceptions about those objects and that the qualities or characteristics which we believe inhere in the objects are merely imputed to them or projected on them by the observer. Recall, for example, that conceptual cognitions often ascertain their objects through the medium of fact-connecting conceptions and that fact-connecting conceptions function by ascribing qualities to objects. These qualities are imputed to the object or designated upon the object from our side, from our store of memories, presumptions, emotions, etc. These qualities do not inhere in the objects themselves. Nāgārjuna intends to show how these conceptions, which are mixed with perceptions, are erroneous and distorted by showing how they are logically unsound in the sense that these conceptions are an interdependent web of definitions, assumptions and so forth. As such, they do not only depend upon the object of perception, but primarily depend on each other. They are thus other than the object of perception, and so must be removed from the cognitive process if one is to be able to develop direct cognition of objects devoid of our assumptions about them.

We will attend to Nāgārjuna's discourse in more detail in section 1-6, but first we must turn to some consideration of the secondary mental factors, especially those which describe how attention operates in the overall cognitive process (section 1-4), and how one can develop the mental concentration (section 1-5) to become aware of this process and so be able to utilize valid conceptual cognitions in the process of developing valid perceptual cognitions.

Section 1-4 Subject; Part 1: Attention

The previous section on perception and conception dealt with material which Tibetan monks generally learn in conjunction with the material in this chapter, the two together being classed as blo rig, "ways of knowing." As the authority for the preceeding material is, ultimately, Dharmakīrti, so the authority for this material is, ultimately, Asaṅga.[1]

At the beginning of section 1-3 I presented a chart which schematized what appeared to be six types of consciousness, and pointed out that in actuality there is only "consciousness" (sems) or (rnam par shes pa, the third limb), and that consciousness always arises and ceases in conjunction with a particular sense organ which serves as the dominant condition for its arising. Thus there only appear to be six different types of consciousness. In section 1-2, where I explained the twelve limb formulation, I also said that consciousness, the third limb, always arises in dependence on karmic formations ('du byed), the second limb. That consciousness (the "name" in "name and form," min dang gzugs) arises in dependence on karmic formations and also arises in conjunction with sense organs is not contradictory, even though the six sense fields (skye mched drug) are the fifth limb in the sequence. This is because the five material sense organs, being material, are part of form, while the nonmaterial sense organ called mind is part of name (because it is actually simply a moment of consciousness preceeding the moment of the arising of a mental consciousness). I also pointed out that the karmic formations quite literally mold the consciousnesses which depend upon them. At this point we will begin to investigate this process in some detail.

The category of teachings referred to as Abhidharma is essentially an elaboration of the karmic formations and consciousness limbs in the twelve limbs formulation, (or the karmic formations skandha and consciousness skandha; recall that the skandha formulation and the twelve limbs formulation analyze many of the same phenomena, but from different perspectives). Within this framework the various consciousnesses are referred to under the rubric "primary consciousness" (gtso sems) or (sems). This is an abstract category because consciousness is always molded by the karmic formations and always arises in conjunction with a sense organ. It cannot be experienced in any other way. When speaking about the way primary consciousness is molded by karmic formations the term "secondary mental factors" (sems 'byung) is utilized to designate the primary consciousness which has been molded by the karmic formations. Geshe Rabten explains the relationship between primary consciousness and secondary mental factors as being like the relationship between a hand (primary consciousness) and the fingers, palm, etc. (secondary mental factors).[2] He further explains "It is not the function of a primary mind [i.e., consciousness] to be specifically concerned with any aspect of the objective field, it is a mere [raw] consciousness of the data presented to it. As we shall see, it is the individual [secondary] mental factors that are responsible for the selection and processing of this data."[3] This is consistent with the twelve limbs formulation because, as we saw, the karmic formations are the traces of previous actions, emotions, etc.; that is, they are the "habits" or "dispositions" of a person, and as such they control cognition, cognition being a process which selects specific aspects out of the overall perceptual field. It is important to recall that the secondary mental factors are merely descriptions of how consciousness functions, they are not entities which act in some way. Thus a secondary mental factor like "sleep" is simply descriptive of a state of consciousness or an activity of consciousness, and the factor of "wisdom" describes consciousness examining the characteristics of a recollected object. These are not something outside of consciousness that do something to consciousness; the mental factors are simply descriptions of how consciousness can be observed to function.

According to Asaṅga's system, there are fifty one secondary mental factors which are arranged into six catagories in accordance with the way they function. Three of these catagories, the wholesome mental factors (dge ba'i sems 'byung), the root afflictions (rtsa ba'i nyon mongs) and the proximate afflictions (nye ba'i nyon mongs), contain thirty seven secondary mental factors which are not directly relevant to the functioning of attention. These thirty seven secondary mental factors make consciousness wholesome (i.e., leading toward peace) or unwholesome (i.e., leading toward suffering). For example, the three poisons at the hub of the wheel of the twelve limbs of dependent origination (delusion, attraction and revulsion) are three of the six root afflictions.

The fourteen secondary mental factors in the other three catagories describe the way in which cognition selects and rejects particular aspects of the data presented to primary consciousness. These three catagories of secondary mental factors are listed below.

THE OMNIPRESENT MENTAL FACTORS

kun 'gro ba'i sems 'byung

feeling	tshor ba
discernment	'du shes
intention	sems pa
contact	reg pa
attention	yid la byed pa

THE OBJECT ASCERTAINING MENTAL FACTORS

yul nges pa'i sems 'byung

aspiration	'dun pa
appreciation	mos pa
recollection	dran pa
concentration	ting nge 'dzin
intelligence/wisdom	shes rab

THE VARIABLE MENTAL FACTORS

gzhan 'gyur ba'i sems 'byung

sleep	gnyid
regret	'gyod pa
general examination	rtog pa
precise analysis	dpyod pa

The omnipresent mental factors and the object ascertaining mental factors are neither wholesome nor unwholesome in and of themselves, whereas the variable mental factors can be either wholesome or unwholesome depending upon circumstance. In this group, sleep and regret are of no particular concern to us, while general examination and precise analysis will be, as these two factors, along with the ten in the previous two catagories, are involved in that aspect of the cognitive process which actually produces the mental images and conceptions discussed in section 1-3.

Contact (also identified as the sixth limb) is a secondary mental factor which indicates that a perceptual object, a sense organ and a primary consciousness have come into *contact*, establishing the basis for the occurrence of a cognition. Feeling (also identified as the seventh limb) is a response of pleasure, pain or indifference; it is a cognition which arises in dependence on consciousness coming into contact with an object. Intention is the orienting of consciousness to the general field of perception; it describes the habitual tendency of consciousness to become involved with and apprehend objects. Geshe Rabten describes it as "the actual principle of activity. It is *karma* itself. Whether an action is mental, vocal or physical, the formative element that is primarily responsible and that accumulates tendencies and imprints on the mind is intention. Thus it acts as a basis for conditioned existence."[4] Attention is the focusing of consciousness on a specific aspect of the general field of perception. Discernment is the identifying and discriminating of that specific aspect of the general field of perception as being one thing rather than another either through the use of signs (mtshan ma), such as labels, or without the use of signs. It is in discernment through the use of signs that the nominal and experiential mental images and the term-connecting and fact-connecting conceptions directly effect cognition. Examples of discernment without signs are the discernment of a child who has not yet learned language and the discernment "of a meditative perception of ultimate truth in which there is no sign of any conditioned phenomenon,"[5] that is, a valid cognition of an accomplished meditator, an Ārya. Aspiration is the taking of a strong interest in the aspect of the general field of perception that has been attended to and discerned as being one thing rather than another. Appreciation is the stabilizing of attention upon the aspect of the perceptual field which has been attended to and discerned. It is the resisting of distraction by other aspects of the perceptual field and serves as the basis for recollection. Recollection is the repeated returning of attention to that aspect of the perceptual field which had earlier been discerned as being one thing rather than another. It serves as a basis for concentration. Concentration is the one-pointed fixing of attention on a specific aspect of the perceptual field. Intelligence or wisdom examines the characteristics or the value of that aspect of the perceptual field being attended to. General examination is the searching for a rough understanding about that aspect of the field of perception which has been discerned by labels or examined by intelligence, while precise analysis is the analyzing of it in some detail.

All these fourteen secondary mental factors function together in the creation of an appearing object (snang yul) within the field of perception. This appearing object is not an actual external object. Rather it is a representation which is constructed by the secondary mental factors operating within the overall cognitive process described in section 1-3. Many of the factors simply describe the way in which cognition is an attending to one aspect of bare perception (a primary mind) over another, thus isolating that aspect as a potential object of perception, and this is determined by various factors such as the power of recollection, concentration, and the karmic traces ('du byed). Furthermore, this aspect of the perceptual field, though it is cognized nonconceptually in bare perception, must be mixed with mental images or concepts in order to be cognized by mental consciousness, and this is a further obscuration. Factors such as discernment describe the way in which an aspect of the perceptual field thus isolated is identified as being a specific object through the use of concepts. Clearly then, the nature of the appearing object which is constructed in this process will to a great extent be determined by the characteristics of the concepts employed in discerning it. These concepts are Nāgārjuna's principle concern in the *Seventy Stanzas*.

Still, it is possible to cultivate one's powers of intelligence/wisdom and concentration so that conceptual cognition can be transformed into valid conceptual cognition (cf. section 1-3). Moreover, as developing one's powers of concentration also makes it possible to discern objects without utilizing signs (mtshan ma med pa'i 'du shes), that is, without imputing labels or concepts to various aspects of the perceptual field, so it is possible to develop valid perceptual cognition. This is bare, direct perception which is devoid of distortion; it is the mode of cognition of the Ārya(s) who have perfected themselves in meditation and moral discipline. These powers of concentration are the topic of the next section.

Section 1-5 Subject; Part 2: Meditation

The practice of meditation can be traced back to the very beginning of the Buddhadharma, for as we saw in section 1-2, Shākyamuni mastered concentration exercises under two different teachers prior to his enlightenment and ascended the eight stages of dhyāna (concentration, bsam gtan) on the evening of his enlightenment. As can be seen from the following description, these stages of dhyāna represent a progressive concentration of the attention and detachment from both physical sense and mental sense experience.

First stage of dhyāna:
Detached from sense-desires, detached (also from the other four) unwholesome states, he dwells in the attainment of the first dhyāna, which is accompanied by applied and discursive thinking, born of detachment, rapturous and joyful.

Second stage of dhyāna:
From the appeasing of applied and discursive thinking, he dwells in the attainment of the second dhyāna, where the inward heart is serene and uniquely exhalted, and which is devoid of applied and

discursive thinking, born of concentration, rapturous and joyful.

Third stage of dhyāna:
Through distaste for rapture he dwells evenmindedly, mindful and clearly conscious; he experiences with this body that joy of which the Ariyans declare, "joyful lives he who is evenminded and mindful."

Fourth stage of dhyāna:
From the forsaking of joy, from the forsaking of pain, from the going to rest of his former gladness and sadness, he dwells in the attainment of the fourth dhyāna, which is neither painful nor pleasureable, — in utter purity of evenmindedness and mindfulness.

Fifth stage of dhyāna:
By passing quite beyond all perceptions of form, by the going to rest of the perceptions of impact, by not attending to the perception of manifoldness, on thinking "endless space," he dwells in the attainment of the station of endless space.

Sixth stage of dhyāna:
By passing quite beyond the station of endless space, on thinking "endless consciousness," he dwells in the attainment of the station of unlimited consciousness.

Seventh stage of dhyāna:
By passing quite beyond the station of unlimited consciousness, on thinking "there is not anything," he dwells in the attainment of the station of nothing whatever.

Eighth stage of dhyāna:
By passing quite beyond the field of nothing whatever, he dwells in the attainment of the station of neither perception nor non-perception.[1]

The purpose of developing such capacity in concentration is not merely to detach the mind from the fetters of worldly existence, which was the purpose of concentration exercises for the Buddha's contemporaries, but rather to have a servicable instrument for developing the direct valid cognitions which would reveal the true nature or existential status of consciousness and its objects. The Buddha recognized that bondage and suffering lay in the perpetuation of ignorance (the first limb of dependent origination), which ignorance is the belief in an actual selfhood or identity or inherent existence in phenomena. He recognized that so long as this erroneous view was held by a being, that being would continue to cycle through the various realms of existence. While it is true that attaining the higher stages of dhyāna refines and detaches the subjective consciousness to the point that it no longer experiences anything unpleasant, yet when a being is no longer meditating, suffering will be experienced because all the ignorant views and karmic formations will regain their power over that being. This is because they are merely suppressed during meditation, they are not rooted out. When that being dies, this ignorance and store of karmic formations will propel it into a new saṃsāric existence. Moreover, even if that being were to spend an entire lifetime on one of the levels of dhyāna and die in such a state, it would merely be reborn in a realm of existence that corresponded to the level of dhyāna it had obtained in life. Such a solitary peace may appear not to be an unpleasant state, but it is still within the saṃsāric cycle, and is not permanent. When that being's stock of merit is exhausted it will have to be reborn in a lower state, and such a state will be attended by suffering.

Only by cutting the source of suffering and bondage off at the root, ignorance, can a being be liberated. To cut off ignorance, one must be able to validly and directly perceive the true nature of those phenomena which are erroneously grasped at by ignorance. In part, this requires developing one's powers of concentrated attention so that one can directly observe the processes of perceptual and conceptual cognition. In this way, for example, inattentive perception (snang la ma nges pa) of the moments of cognition would be converted into attentive perception of the moments of cognition. As we saw in section 1-3, such a bare cognition would be valid. One could actually have bare perceptions of phenomena and see how it was that mental images were combined with these bare perceptions in the production of erroneous conceptual consciousnesses. Such a direct perception would contribute to liberation, but even it would not eradicate the store of ignorant views about phenomena which are the source for the production of the mental images. Such ignorant views can only be dispelled by their opposite, wisdom, i.e., erroneous views can only be rooted out by valid inferences (rjes dpag tshad ma) and mistaken perceptions can only be rooted out by valid perceptions (mngon sum tshad ma). The meditative path, as described in Tibetan Prāsaṅgika, combines these two operations.[2]

The commentary to *Seventy Stanzas* 62 presents a summary of the meditative path within the context of developing a consciousness which can directly and validly cognize the emptiness of phenomena. Here reasoning is an initial step on the meditative path because for a person without training the emptiness of phenomena is not something that can be seen directly, and the meditator must know what to meditate upon. The kārikā(s) of the *Seventy Stanzas* describe the actual nature of phenomena; to study and comprehend them is to replace mistaken conceptual cognitions (rtog pa log shes) first with correct beliefs (yid dpyod) and then with valid conceptual cognitions (rjes dpag tshad ma). The intense intellectual effort made to comprehend the reasonings of the kārikā(s) and develop valid conceptual cognitions is referred to as an analytic meditation (dpyad sgom). This sort of meditation is a concentration of mental consciousness (yid kyi rnams par shes pa) on an idea and is discursive rather than one pointed. Utilizing the mental factor (sems 'byung) of recollection (dran pa) one returns over and over again to the reasonings in the kārikā(s) and in this way cultivates the mental factor of intelligence or wisdom (shes rab). When wisdom is sharp one can convert the correct beliefs which are based upon the study of the kārikā(s) into valid conceptual cognitions. The mental images (don spyi) of the valid conceptual cognitions developed in this analytic meditation are then utilized as the objects of attention in the practice of stabilizing meditations ('jog sgom), which are onepointed.

In the next stage of the actual meditative path one seeks to develop what is called calm abiding (zhi gnas) because upon the calming of the distractions originating in the five material senses the mental consciousness abides onepointedly and nondiscursively on a mental object of observation (in this case the mental image of emptiness). Here one utilizes the mental factor of recollectedness in regards to an object of meditation to develop concentration (ting nge 'dzin) on it, which is an actual onepointedness of consciousness. Over time one's calm abiding becomes more stable, clear, intense and serviceable. When not actually performing this stabilizing meditation one would return to an analytic meditation on emptiness to further cultivate valid conceptual cognitions of emptiness. Initially these two are done as separate meditative sessions because the discursiveness of the analytic meditation would interfere with the cultivation of onepointedness in the stabilizing meditation and the onepointedness of the stabilizing meditation would interfere with the discursive reasoning process in the analytic meditation which develops the valid conceptual cognitions about emptiness.

The next stage on the meditative path is the development of special insight (lhag mthong). Initially one strengthens and harmonizes the stabilizing meditations and the analytic meditations by alternating between the two of them. Eventually each one reinforces and induces the other; the onepointedness developed in the stabilizing meditations makes the analytic meditations onepointed, penetrating and powerful, while the understanding of emptiness developed in the analytic meditations makes the stabilizing meditations firmer and more intense. At this point one has actually obtained calm abiding and special insight and one's experience of emptiness goes beyond mere conceptualizations. Upon their union, with emptiness as their object, the Path of Preparation (sbyor lam) is obtained.

There are four stages on the Path of Preparation in which the meditator successively removes the experienced distinctions between subject (consciousness) and object (mental image of emptiness) and then removes the mental image of emptiness itself. When this happens and the meditator directly perceives emptiness itself without the mediation of a mental image he is said to have entered the Path of Seeing (mthong lam) and is called an Ārya. Here the meditator has developed valid perceptions (mngon sum tshad ma) which last longer than one sixty fifth of a finger snap.

On the Path of Seeing the meditator removes all the conceptions of inherent existence of phenomena which are based on erroneous systems of teaching, language and social convention. This all happens in the course of one meditative session. However, the conceptions of inherent existence of phenomena which are innate to beings from beginningless time still remain, and these are to be removed on the next level, the Path of Meditation (sgom lam). It should be noted that the Ārya only has valid perceptual cognitions while actually meditating. When he or she arises from meditation he or she will see a world of conventional appearances; that is, phenomena will appear to exist inherently until all the innate conceptions of inherent existence are removed.

The various types of innate conception of inherent existence which are removed on the Path of Meditation are arranged according to the nine levels of consciousness, by which are meant ordinary consciousness plus the consciousness of the eight dhyāna(s). As indicated earlier, these are not only concentrated states of consciousness but also places of rebirth for those beings with strong powers of concentration. Mere power of concentration and the ability to attain one of these high dhyāna(s) cannot bring about liberation because of the innate conceptions of inherent existence of phenomena which remain even in these states. Now, on the Path of Meditation, the Ārya removes all these innate conceptions of inherent existence. When these innate conceptions of inherent existence have been removed the meditator obtains the Path of No More Learning (mi slob lam), i.e., Buddhahood.[3] Finally, with Buddhahood, both the conventional appearance of phenomena and their emptiness, i.e., the two truths (conventional truth: kun rdzob bden pa and ultimate truth: don dam bden pa) appear simultaneously (which is the definition of omniscience), and there is no distinction to be made between a period of meditation and a period of nonmeditation — all a Buddha's cognitions are direct and valid.

Section 1-6 Object

Up to now we have been discussing the process of perception and the way it can be transformed through meditation. In explaining this perceptual process the Buddhist epistemologists point out that what we take for a concrete perceived object with the appearance of an existence which is external to the perceiving subject is, in actuality, a mentally constructed image (an appearing object, snang yul), whose characteristics depend upon both external factors and subjective factors. Some of these subjective factors are the actual process of perception itself, while others are emotions and desires. An additional key subjective factor which effects the construction of perceptual objects is the imputation of concepts upon the object being formed; i.e., the mixing of concepts or mental images with the objects presented in bare perception, which was discussed in section 1-3.

Recall that in the formulation of the twelve limbs of dependent origination the six sense fields arise in dependence on mind and body, which arise in dependence on consciousness, which arises in dependence on karmic formations, which arise in dependence on ignorance. The fifty one secondary mental factors elaborated by Asaṅga are a systematic description of the linkage between karmic formations and consciousness. As consciousness is always "consciousness of something," so Asaṅga describes in detail how this "consciousness of some*thing*" is molded by habits, conceptions and emotions — the karmic formations that consciousness arises in dependence upon. The perceptual scheme elaborated by Dharmakīrti is a systematic description of the linkage between the six sense fields and consciousness through the medium of mind and body; it describes the process of perceiving the some*thing*. That is, Dharmakīrti demonstrates how perception is a linkage between the consciousness-molded-by-karmic-formations and the perceptual field. In dependence upon both of these linkages, contact arises: an object is actually cognized. Here we understand "cognized" to mean that in the perceptual process an object is created in a consciousness which functions in dependence on the karmic formations.

The karmic formations themselves arise in dependence on ignorance, which is defined as an incorrect knowledge about the status of phenomena.[1] It is this incorrect knowledge which at root is responsible for the discerning ('du shes) of objects in the perceptual field in the first place. On the other hand, intelligence or wisdom (shes rab) examines the characteristics or value of the objects perceived, and cultivating wisdom about objects and the process of cognition itself can serve as an antidote to ignorance. When ignorance is converted to correct knowledge, fallacious imputations cease and the whole twelve limb cycle is cut at its root, so suffering ceases. Saṁsāra becomes nirvāṇa as objects are perceived for what they actually are. It is this ignorance which is Nāgārjuna's particular concern in the *Seventy Stanzas;* his intention is to provide its antidote through the means of his logical discourse which first establishes correct beliefs (yid dpyod) and later develops wisdom. Based upon these one can develop valid cognitions (tshad ma) about the nature of phenomena which results in a transformation of the karmic formations and so the entire perceptual process which depends upon them is also transformed. As the creation of objects in the perceptual process is transformed, what had previously appeared as saṁsāra now appears as nirvāṇa.

Nāgārjuna's whole position is summed up in stanzas two and three of the *Seventy Stanzas*, which I abridge below:

> All phenomena which are the subject of this treatise are similar to nirvāṇa because all phenomena are devoid of inherent existence. What is the reason for this? It is because the inherent existence of all phenomena is not to be found in causes, conditions, aggregations or individualities. Thus all phenomena are devoid of inherent existence and are empty.

To boil this down to its essentials, Nāgārjuna is simply making the following basic formulation: All phenomena are devoid of inherent existence. The entire *Seventy Stanzas* is just an elaboration of how specific phenomena which are of particular concern to Buddhists are empty (shūnya, stong pa) of inherent existence (svabhāva, rang bzhin).

To understand Nāgārjuna's discourse, it will be useful to begin by examining the three elements of the above summary in turn: phenomena, inherent existence and devoidness/emptiness (they are two ways of saying the same thing).

"Phenomenon" or "thing" or "functional phenomenon" or "functional thing" (cf., stanza 16) (vastu, dngos po) is a term which designates an object of cognition. It is equivalent to an object condition (dmigs rkyen), which Candrakīrti defines as a support or basis (ālambana, dmigs pa) for the arising of the three poisons.[2] As we saw in section 1-3, a phenomenon (object condition) can be an external object, or it can be a bare perceptual cognition, or it can be a conceptual cognition, for any of these can serve as the basis for the arising of the three poisons.

"Inherent existence" (svabhāva, rang bzhin) is a term which refers to the pervasion of the phenomenon by a certain ontological status: existence. This concept is best understood by breaking the Sanskrit and Tibetan words into their components: "sva-" and "rang" correspond to "self" or "own" in English, while "-bhāva" and "bzhin" correspond to "being" or "existence" in English. The "own-being" or "self-existence" designated by the terms svabhāva and rang bzhin is an *existence* which inhers in something it*self*, a *being* which inhers in something on its *own*. That is to say, this term designates an actual independent existential status which is a characteristic of the phenomenon in and of itself. This existential status should not be something that is imputed to the phenomenon from the subjective side ("from our side," as the Tibetans would say), nor should this existential status depend on any factor which is not a part of the object itself. Rather, this existence must be a status which inhers in the very nature of the phenomenon: this is what is meant when it is said that this existential status must be independent. "Inherent existence" refers to the very essence of the phenomenon, that which makes it *be*.

Svabhāva/rang bzhin has been translated by a number of English equivalents; we have chosen "inherent existence" rather than some other possible terms because it is precisely Nāgārjuna's point that existential characteristics are not independent and do not inhere in phenomena but rather are dependent because they are imputed upon phenomena which in and of themselves actually lack those characteristics. This is what is meant by the term "devoid" in the summary statement above. It is a simple negation, which is formulated throughout the *Seventy Stanzas* in the following ways: phenomena lack inherent existence, phenomena are devoid of inherent existence, phenomena are empty of inherent existence, phenomena are empty, phenomena do not exist (this last statement being a kind of shorthand for "do not exist inherently" or "do not exist as they appear"). These all mean the same thing. However, this does not mean that phenomena have no existence whatsoever. If this were the case, what would serve as the basis for the false imputation of inherent existence? Since existence does not inhere in this basis, but is imputed to it in the process of cognition, so Nāgārjuna says that this basis does not exist inherently, or exists non-inherently (rang bzhin med), or more simply, that this basis is empty (shūnya, stong pa). This is the actual status of phenomena in and of themselves. To translate svabhāva/rang bzhin as "own-being" or "self-existence" would therefore also require formulating its negation as "non-own-being" or "non-self-existence," which are obscure in English, not to mention clumsy. On the other hand, "non-inherent-existence" is precisely what Nāgārjuna means when he states that phenomena are empty of svabhāva/rang bzhin. That is, the actual status of phenomena is that they are full of non-inherent existence, they actually exist non-inherently and they appear to us as being full of our imputations.

How is it possible that existence does not inhere in the objects of perception? Recall that typically we do not cognize actual objects in and of themselves, but rather cognize conceptions or representations of objects in consciousness; that is, a mixture of bare perceptions and mental images. These images are pervaded by concepts and the ordinary person is not aware of the difference between the bare image and the concepts which pervade it. As Nāgārjuna points out in stanza 27, "Without depending on the defined one cannot establish a definition and without considering the definition one cannot establish the defined." That is to say, although it is possible to intellectually consider an object and its characteristics as being two different things, in fact we only cognize them in an interdependent fashion. When we cognize an object it appears to us that it exists, but actually existence is a characteristic which defines an object, just as non-existence is a characteristic which defines an object. Existence or non-existence are concepts or characteristics imputed upon bare perceptions in the perceptual process of forming an object.

Indeed, if one considers how one develops the belief that existence is an attribute of an object, that existence inhers in an object, it becomes apparent that one develops such a belief in dependence on that object having a certain aggregation of characteristics. For example, if I listen for the singing of my pet bird and I do not hear any sound, I may say that there is no singing. That is, the singing is non-existent. I can make such a statement because in the past I heard my bird singing, but in the present it is not singing. The singing has ceased, so it is non-existent in the present, but it occurred in the past (or "arose" in the past, as Nāgārjuna would say), at which time it was existent. Now this example demonstrates how the characteristic of existence is dependent upon other characteristics, such as the arising, enduring and ceasing of a phenomenon over periods of time. A sound must arise in the present for it to exist; "presentness" and "arising" must be characteristics of a sound in order for me to cognize the sound as existing. If these characteristics are lacking, then I cannot cognize a sound as existing, rather I cognize it as non-existing. In this way existence is a characteristic which is imputed upon a phenomenon if it is arising in the present, but existence is not something which inhers in a phenomenon itself, such as singing, for if the characteristics "present" and "arising" are separated from the phenomenon itself, the phenomenon can no longer be said to exist.

Now, it may seem that this is just an intellectual exercise, for even if one accepts that existence is merely designated upon appearing phenomena, still something does appear in perception. Nāgārjuna does not refute this. Indeed, this is precisely his point, and he refers to this mere appearance as the true status of phenomena; the ultimate truth (don dam dben pa) about phenomena is that they are mere appearances which are empty of the characteristics we attribute to them, while the conventional truth (kun rdzob bden pa) about phenomena is the fact of their erroneous appearance to ordinary beings.

Moreover, existence is not the only characteristic we attribute or impute to phenomena. In the above example of the singing bird our analysis forced us to consider singing as a phenomenon which arises, endures and ceases over the past and present. Even if we are not considering the existential status of a phenomenon, still we typically perceive it as having characteristics such as arising or enduring, or as having shape and color and so forth. We naturally consider that these characteristics inhere in the phenomenon itself, but do they? If enduring were a characteristic that inhered in a phenomenon then it would be independent of anything else, such as the characteristics of arising and ceasing. But we can only know that something endures to the extent that we have the ideas of arising and ceasing, for enduring only has meaning in relation to these two, it depends upon them. Moreover, a phenomenon can't actually endure unless it has previously arisen. And what phenomenon would cease if it had not arisen? Furthermore, these occur over time. For something to cease in the present it must have arisen in the past. But the past is only the past in dependence on the present. Thus not only the concepts "arising," "enduring" and "ceasing" but also their phenomenal referents are mutually interdependent. Thus they are not independent characteristics which inhere in phenomena.

To use the example of shape and color, we seem to cognize a thing as having both shape and color, even if we cognize it barely. But can a phenomenon have shape without color or color without shape? They seem to be different, and the modes of describing one cannot be used for describing another. We cannot use terms such as red or blue to distinguish between rectangles and circles, for any shape can have any color. Such characteristics only are what they are in relation to each other, they are not what they are in relation to the phenomena which they are supposed to characterize. Thus these characteristics cannot be said to exist independently of each other nor, as we have seen from stanza 27 of the *Seventy Stanzas*, can they be said to exist independently of the objects they characterize. That is to say, these characteristics are only what they are in dependence on each other and in dependence on the objects they are supposed to characterize.

Do they, then, actually exist? Nāgārjuna devotes most of the *Seventy Stanzas* to this question. As he shows in example after example, these characteristics exist in dependence on each other, they do not inhere in phenomena but are merely imputed upon phenomena in the perceptual process. Yet he also demonstrates that it cannot be said that they do not exist, for they do exist, but dependently and non-inherently.

This question about the existential status of phenomena and their characteristics is relevant because Nāgārjuna is, afterall, teaching within the context of the Buddhist tradition. His purpose, like that of all Buddhist teachers, is to show a path for the liberation from suffering. The twelve limbs of dependent origination formulation shows that the source of suffering is ignorant grasping after phenomena, but what is it we are grasping after? We grasp after phenomena to satisfy desires and obtain happiness or else to avoid suffering. But we do not grasp after phenomena in and of themselves independent of their characteristics. Indeed it is the characteristics of phenomena which we presume will satisfy us. It is, for example, the taste of food and the feeling of a full stomach which is gratifying, not the "stuff" of the food in itself. But, as Nāgārjuna demonstrates, these characteristics are imputed on phenomena, they do not inhere in phenomena themselves. Yet they are not independent of phenomena, for there must be a basis upon which the imputation can be made.

Here Nāgārjuna shows us the fundamental distortion in the cognitive process which sets the saṁsāric cycle of the twelve limbs in motion and drags beings through the various realms of existence. This fundamental distortion is the tendency to take an extreme view toward phenomena, that is, to overestimate their natures. This extreme view or overestimation is that phenomena are independent, self-sufficient entities which bear their own characteristics independently of the preceiving subject; that is, the view that their characteristics exist in or inhere in them independently of any other subjective or external factors. Due to this extreme view attachment or revulsion for objects is developed and peace is lost. Destroy this extreme view and peace (nirvāṇa) will be gained. As Nāgārjuna says in stanza 65:

> Understanding the non-inherent existence of things means seeing the reality [i.e., emptiness] which eliminates ignorance about the reality of things. This brings about the cessation of ignorantly grasping at an apparently true existence. From that the twelve limbs of dependent origination cease.

Finally, we should recollect that there are both external phenomena and internal phenomena toward which we can develop extreme views. Indeed, grasping after internal phenomena based on extreme views about the so called "person" produces the greatest amount of suffering, for external objects are only of value to us in relation to that very "us." To crush extreme views about internal phenomena and destroy the grasping after internal phenomena Nāgārjuna analyzes the complex of the six sense fields, six sense organs and six consciousnesses, as well as the twelve limbs in the twelve limbs of dependent origination. As he shows for each scheme, its elements arise in dependence on each other in an inextricable way. For example, there is no consciousness without an object basis for consciousness, nor vice versa. Since they both arise in dependence on each other, so neither exists inherently. Similarly, no single limb in the twelve limb scheme arises independently of any other limb. Thus all object bases, limbs and consciousnesses lack inherent existence and only exist in dependence on each other. They are merely transitory phenomena flashing into awareness and immediately disintegrating. Yet they are not mere hallucinations without any basis whatsoever. When this real nature of phenomena is seen, grasping after them will naturally cease. Key among these internal phenomena are consciousness and cognizing, for these are the basic, fundamental phenomena which we grasp after. When such grasping ceases, cognizing goes on placidly, consciousness remains clear and lucid and all phenomena are seen to be "... similar to nirvāṇa because all phenomena are devoid of inherent existence."[3]

Chapter Two
The Seventy Stanzas on Emptiness

Section 2-1 Seventy Stanzas Explaining How Phenomena Are Empty of Inherent Existence

Prostration is made to the Youthful Manjushrī.

[1] "Arising," "enduring," and "disintegrating;" "existing" and "non-existing;" "inferior," "middling," and "superior" do not have true existence. These terms are used by the Buddha in accordance with worldly conventions.

[2] All phenomena must have either self-existence or non-self-existence. There is no phenomenon which is other than these two, nor are there any expressions which do not come under these two catagories. All phenomena which are the subject of this treatise are similar to nirvāṇa because all phenomena are devoid of inherent existence.

[3] What is the reason for this? It is because the inherent existence of all phenomena is not to be found in causes, conditions, aggregations or individualities. Thus all phenomena are devoid of inherent existence and are empty.

[4] Some assert that a result already exists inherently in the nature of its cause; but then it cannot arise because it already exists. Others assert that a result exists inherently but not in the nature of its cause; so it cannot arise because it is not in the nature of its cause. Yet others assert that a result both does and does not exist inherently in its cause; but then they are asserting contradictory views about an object because an object cannot simultaneously both exist and not exist. Because phenomena do not arise inherently so also they do not endure or cease inherently.

[5] Whatsoever has already arisen will not be able to arise. Whatsoever has not arisen will not arise. Either a phenomenon has already arisen or else it will arise; there is no other possibility beyond these two. Whatever is in the process of arising should have already arisen or else it will arise in the future.

[6] The cause of a result which already exists is similar to that which is not a cause. Also in the case where a result does not already exist, then its cause will be similar to that which is not a cause. A phenomenon should be either existent or non-existent but cannot be both non-existent and not-non-existent because these two are contradictory. Therefore it is not suitable to assert that there is either an inherently existing cause or an inherently existing result in the three times.

[7] Without one there cannot be many and without many it is not possible to refer to one. Therefore one and many arise dependently and such phenomena do not have the sign of inherent existence.

[8] The twelve limbs of dependent origination result in suffering: since the twelve limbs and suffering do not arise independently of each other, they don't exist inherently. Furthermore, it is not acceptable to assert that the twelve

limbs are based on a single moment of a mind nor on successive moments of a mind, as such moments arise dependently and do not exist inherently.

[9] Because contaminated things arise in dependence on one another they do not exist inherently as permanent phenomena nor do they exist inherently as impermanent phenomena; neither as phenomena with self-nature nor without self-nature; neither as pure nor impure; neither as blissful nor as suffering. It is thus that the four distortions do not exist as qualities which inhere in phenomena, but rather are imputed to phenomena.

[10] There are no four distortions which exist inherently and thus there can be no ignorance arising from them. Because that ignorance does not exist inherently it cannot give birth to karmic formations, which means karmic formations will not arise and so also the remaining limbs too.

[11] Ignorance cannot originate as a cause except in dependence on the karmic formations. Also, the karmic formations cannot originate except in dependence on their cause, which is ignorance. Because ignorance and karmic formations are interrelated as cause and effect so these two are known by a valid cognizer not to exist inherently.

[12] By itself none of the twelve limbs can originate inherently, but must depend on the remaining limbs. How then can one limb produce another limb? Moreover, because one limb has originated as a cause in dependence on the other limbs, so how can it act as a condition for the origination of results such as the other limbs?

[13] The father is not the son and the son is not the father. These two are mutually not non-existent and the two of them cannot arise simultaneously. It is likewise with the

twelve dependent limbs.

[14] Just as in a dream, happiness and suffering depend on dream objects and upon awakening these objects are known not to actually exist, likewise any phenomenon which arises in dependence on another dependent phenomenon should be known not to exist in the manner of its appearance.

[15] Vaibhāṣika: If you assert that phenomena don't exist inherently then you are asserting that they don't exist at all. So how can you make distinctions like inferior, middling and superior or that there are different beings in the six realms of existence? How then can you assert the manifestation of a result which arises from causes?

[16] Response: When you assert that phenomena exist inherently you are asserting that they do not originate in dependence on causes and conditions and thus that phenomena actually do not exist. For if phenomena do not depend on causes and conditions, then they should have independent existence throughout the three times. Therefore there cannot be any inherent existence for functional phenomena which arise from causes and conditions or non-functional phenomena which do not arise from causes and conditions, and there cannot be any third mode of existence for phenomena.

[17] Opponent: If phenomena do not exist inherently, how can you use terms to refer to their own characteristics or their characteristics in relation to other phenomena or non-functional phenomena? Response: Although phenomena lack inherent existence, still we can use terms like own-characteristics, other-characteristics and non-functional phenomena for although these are unfindable upon analysis, still, like the objects of a dream they appear to have existence to ordinary perception. So the way they

exist and the way they appear are different and these conventional existences are called distortions or false.

[18] Hīnayānist: If phenomena are devoid of inherent existence then they will be completely non-existent like the horns of a rabbit, and so there can be no occurrence of their arising or their cessation. As Buddha has spoken about arising and cessation, they must exist, so how can things be devoid of inherent existence?

[19] Response: An object cannot simultaneously arise as a functional phenomenon and cease as a non-functional phenomenon. If a non-functional phenomenon does not exist then a functional phenomenon cannot exist because an object cannot arise and endure as a functional phenomenon without depending on its cessation as a non-functional phenomenon, or else it would exist at all times. If a non-functional phenomenon which is different from a functional phenomenon does not exist then it is impossible for a functional phenomenon to exist.

[20] If there is no arising and enduring, which are functional phenomena, then there can be no disintegration or cessation, which are non-functional phenomena; so the latter would be completely non-existent. If a phenomenon were to exist inherently it must have arisen from its own nature or from some other nature, but it cannot arise from its own nature and because a phenomenon cannot have a different nature than its cause, so it cannot arise from some other nature which has inherent existence. Because of that, a functional phenomenon cannot exist inherently and because a functional phenomenon cannot exist inherently, so a non-functional phenomenon cannot exist inherently.

[21] If a phenomenon were to exist inherently it should be permanent. If a phenomenon were to disintegrate completely then you must accept the annihilationist view. If a

phenomenon were to exist inherently it would either exist permanently or else undergo complete disintegration: it cannot occur in a way which is different than these two. Therefore one should not assert that a phenomenon has inherent existence.

[22] Opponent: Because of continuity there is no danger of the two extreme views. Acting as a cause of another causal phenomenon the original causal phenomenon ceases to exist. Reply: As explained before, the cause and the result, like a functional phenomenon and a non-functional phenomenon, cannot arise with inherent existence either simultaneously or sequentially. In your view their lack of inherent existence makes them completely non-existent, in which case you cannot assert their continuity or that of the moments between them. Therefore the faults of the two extremes remain in your view.

[23] Opponent: When Buddha explained the path to liberation he spoke about arising and disintegration, so they must have true existence. Response: It is true that Buddha spoke about arising and disintegration, but they are devoid of inherent existence. For that reason the way they appear and the way they exist are dissimilar, and they appear in a deceptive way to the world.

[24] Opponent: If arising and disintegration do not exist then suffering can not exist, so what cessation will bring forth nirvāṇa? But because nirvāṇa can be attained that means there is suffering which has inherent existence and therefore there is arising with inherent existence and disintegration with inherent existence. Response: Nirvāṇa refers to that state where suffering does not arise with inherent existence and does not cease with inherent existence. Don't we call that state the naturally abiding nirvāṇa? Therefore arising and disintegration do not exist inherently.

[25] You have accepted that the extinction of the continuation of suffering is nirvāṇa, in which case you have held an annihilationist view. And if you modify your position and assert that nirvāṇa is a state where suffering has inherent existence and has not been extinguished, then you accept permanent suffering which even includes the state of nirvāṇa, which is an eternalist view. Therefore you cannot assert that nirvāṇa refers to a state where suffering is a non-functional phenomenon which has been extinguished nor can you assert that nirvāṇa refers to a state where suffering is a functional phenomenon which has not been extinguished. These two assertions about nirvāṇa are not appropriate. Therefore nirvāṇa refers to that state where suffering does not arise with inherent existence and does not cease with inherent existence.

[26] If you assert a cessation that is different than a functional phenomenon then you are asserting a cessation which does not depend on a functional phenomenon and which exists inherently and permanently. Because we have refuted the inherent existence of a functional phenomenon and also the inherent existence of a non-functional phenomenon which depends on a functional phenomenon, so here a cessation cannot have independent existence and so it cannot exist inherently or permanently.

[27] Without depending on the defined one cannot establish a definition and without considering the definition one cannot establish the defined. As they depend on each other, they have not arisen by themselves, so therefore the defined and the definition are devoid of inherent existence and also they do not exist inherently in a mutually dependent way, so none of them can be used to establish the inherent existence of another one.

[28] Following the logic of this explanation of mutually

dependent origination one cannot use the cause of a result to prove that the result has inherent existence because the cause of the result originates in dependence on the result and so is devoid of inherent existence. The same applies to all the pairs such as feeling and the one who feels or seeing and the seer, and so forth. Taking these as examples one should understand how all the pairs are explained as being devoid of inherent existence because they originate in mutual dependence.

[29] Time does not exist inherently because the three periods of time do not maintain continuity by themselves, but are dependent on each other. If the three times were to have inherent existence in a mutually dependent way, then we could not make distinctions between them, but because we can make distinctions so time itself cannot be established as having inherent existence. Because time does not have inherent existence, the functional basis on which the three times is imputed cannot have inherent existence, so therefore the three times do not have inherent existence and are merely imputed by concepts.

[30] Following the reasoning just given, the three characteristics of a composite phenomenon which are arising, enduring and ceasing are unfindable upon ultimate analysis even for you, so then a functional phenomenon which is characterized by these three attributes is also unfindable, in which case the functional basis of a composite phenomenon becomes unfindable. So when a composite phenomenon cannot exist inherently, how can a non-composite phenomenon which depends on a composite phenomenon have inherent existence in the least.

[31] At the point of its complete disintegration does a phenomenon disintegrate which has already disintegrated or at that point does a phenomenon disintegrate which has not yet disintegrated? In the first case the process of disintegration is complete, so this cannot be accepted. In the

second case it is free from the function of disintegration, so this cannot be accepted. The same applies to enduring and arising. If a phenomenon were to endure at that point when it has already endured then the process of enduring is complete and we cannot say that it is enduring at that point. And a phenomenon which has not endured cannot be accepted as enduring at that point because it is free from the function of enduring. If a phenomenon were to arise at the point of arising which has already arisen then the process of arising is already complete, so this cannot be accepted. And if a phenomenon were to arise at that point which has not arisen then that case is not acceptable, because it is non-existent.

[32] If we examine composite phenomena and non-composite phenomena then we cannot find them as one, because then we cannot differentiate between these two types of phenomena, and we cannot find them as many, because then these two would be completely unrelated. If a composite phenomenon is asserted to exist, then it cannot arise because it is already existent and if it is asserted not to exist, then it cannot arise because it is non-existent. If it is asserted to be both existent and non-existent, this is not possible because such a state is contradictory. Every different type of phenomenon is included within this criterion of non-inherent existence.

[33] Opponent: The Peerless Subduer has taught that there is continuity in the flow of actions. Likewise, he has taught about the nature of actions and their results. He has also taught that the results of actions performed by an individual sentient being must be experienced by him and that whatever actions are performed are certain to bear fruit. For these four reasons actions have inherent existence.

[34] Reply: Buddha taught that actions do not exist inherently and so they cannot arise inherently. Although ac-

tions do not exist inherently, they will not be wasted but it is certain that they will bear fruit. From these actions arise consciousness, name and form, and the rest of the limbs of dependent origination. Conception of self is generated through focusing on the person who is merely imputed upon these dependent limbs. Also, it arises from the pre-conception which takes improper objects and overestimates them.

[35] If actions were to have inherent existence then they would not be impermanent but would have the nature of permanence, and then the body which results from those actions would also be permanent. If actions were to be permanent then they could not give rise to suffering, which is the ripening of actions. If actions were non-changing then they would have the nature of permanence and then they would have self-existence. But then Buddha would not have taught about the lack of self-nature.

[36] If actions were to exist at the time of conditions, those actions could not arise from those conditions. And if conditions do not have the potential to give rise to actions, then actions cannot arise from conditions because those conditions are similar to non-conditions. Because actions cannot arise even slightly from non-conditions, so therefore all composite phenomena are like an illusion, and a gandharva town and a mirage, and therefore they lack inherent existence.

[37] Actions are caused by delusions. Our body arises from the nature of delusions and actions. Because the cause of the body is actions, and actions arise from delusions, so therefore these three are devoid of inherent existence.

[38] When actions do not have inherent existence there will be no person to perform actions. Because both of them do not exist, results do not exist. When there are no results there will be no person to experience those results physical-

ly and mentally. Because of that reason that actions do not exist inherently, so all phenomena are devoid of inherent existence.

[39] If one understands how actions are devoid of inherent existence, then he sees the suchness of actions. When he has seen suchness he will have eliminated ignorance and when there is no ignorance then the actions which are caused by ignorance cannot arise in him, and so the results of actions such as consciousness and so forth up to aging and dealth will not be experienced by him. When consciousness ceases to exist the dependent limb of aging and death cannot occur; thus he will attain the state of liberation free from aging and death.

[40-41] Through his miraculous powers, Tathāgata the Subduer emitted an emanation and that emanation emitted another emanation. As the emanation emitted by the Tathāgata is devoid of inherent existence, it is hardly necessary to say that the emanation emitted by the emanation is also devoid of inherent existence. When we say that these two emanations do not exist inherently, that does not mean that they are completely non-existent but rather that both of them, just like actions and the one who performs actions, merely exist through terms because they are separated from the nature of inherent existence. They do exist, but merely through imputation by thought in a deceptive way.

[42] The person who performs actions is said to be similar to the emanation emitted by the Tathāgata because he is led by ignorance. And so his actions are said to be similar to the emanation emitted by the emanation. All of these are devoid of inherent existence, though they do have a slight existence as mere imputations supported by terms and concepts.

[43] If actions were to have the nature of inherent existence, then they would be permanent. But if actions were

permanent then they would not depend on a person, and if there were no person to perform actions, then actions would not exist. In that case, nirvāṇa, which is the state of cessation of delusions and actions, could not be attained. If actions did not exist through mere terms and concepts then their ripening results such as happiness and suffering could not arise.

[44] Whatever is said by the Buddha has the two truths as its chief underlying thought; it is hard to understand and must be interpreted in this light. When the Buddha says "existence" his chief underlying thought is conventional existence; when he says "non-existence" his chief underlying thought is non-inherent existence; when he says "existence-and-non-existence" his chief underlying thought is conventional-existence-and-non-inherent-existence as a mere object of examination.

[45] Neither does inherently existent form, having the nature of elements, arise from elements nor from itself and not even from others. Therefore, it does not exist, does it?

[46] A form cannot have the fourfold nature of the elements because if the form has four elements then it will be fourfold and the four elements cannot have a singular form or else they will become one like form, so how can form arise from the four great elements as its cause?

[47] Form is not apprehended as inherently existing, so therefore the form does not exist inherently. If it is said that the inherent existence of form is understood by the mind which apprehends it, then such a mind does not exist inherently because it has arisen from causes and conditions so it cannot be used as a reason for proving the inherent existence of a form.

[48] If a mind apprehends a form with inherent existence

then the mind will apprehend its own nature. Such a mind has arisen from causes and conditions, so it is a dependent arising which lacks inherent existence. In the same way, form does not exist truly, so how can that mind apprehend a form with true existence?

[49] The kind of form, which has arisen but not ceased to exist, that I have explained is not apprehended by each moment of the mind in the present. Therefore, how can such a mind apprehend forms of the past and also the future?

[50] In all times color and shape do not exist as two different things. If they were to exist as two different things then a mind could apprehend shape without considering color or color without considering shape. Because these two do not exist as two different things, so therefore there is not a mind which apprehends shape without taking color into consideration nor color without taking shape into consideration. In the world, a form is known to be singular; if its shape and color were to exist as two different things then the form would appear to the world as two instead of one.

[51] The eye has no consciousness because the eye is a form but eye consciousness is formless and that which is formless cannot adhere to form. In the same way the form which is observed has no eye consciousness, nor is it between eye and form. Because eye consciousness is generated in dependence on eye and form, if it is apprehended as having inherent existence, that is a mistaken conception.

[52] When the eye does not see itself, how can it see forms? Therefore the eye and the forms do not have self-existence and the remaining entrances should be understood in the same way.

[53] The eye is devoid of its own self-existent nature. It is

also devoid of the self-existent nature of an other. In the same way, form is devoid of its own self-existent nature as well as that of another. And it is the same with the rest of the entrances.

[54] When any of the six internal entrances arises simultaneously with contact, at that time the rest of the entrances will be devoid of the nature of contact. The rest of the entrances which are devoid of the nature of contact do not depend on the nature of contact. That which is not devoid of the nature of contact will not depend on that which is devoid of the nature of contact.

[55] The eye, eye consciousness and its object arise and immediately disintegrate, so they cannot exist as abiding in their natures and so those three cannot assemble. When these three cannot assemble, contact cannot exist and if contact cannot exist, so there cannot be feeling.

[56] Consciousness arises in dependence on internal and external entrances. Because consciousness arises in dependence on the entrances, so it is like a mirage and an illusion which are devoid of inherent existence.

[57] Consciousness cannot arise without taking its object, so it depends on the object of knowledge. The object of knowledge cannot arise without depending on the consciousness which apprehends it, and therefore because they exist in a mutually dependent way both of them lack inherent existence. The object of knowledge and the apprehension of the object do not exist inherently, therefore the person who knows the object does not exist inherently.

[58] Buddha has seen no essence in composite phenomena with inherent existence so he said that all composite phenomena are impermanent, so therefore they are devoid of inherent existence, or because he said that all composite phenomena are impermanent, so how could they

exist inherently in the nature of permanent phenomena? If phenomena were to have inherent existence they should either be permanent or impermanent: how can there be phenomena which are both permanent and impermanent at the same time?

[59] Through superimposition one develops the three distorted preconceptions toward pleasing, repulsive and neutral objects, which respectively cause attachment, hatred and closed-mindedness. Because they arise in dependence on these conditions, the essential nature of attachment, hatred and closed-mindedness is without inherent existence.

[60] A pleasing object does not exist inherently because some persons develop attachment towards it, others develop hatred towards it, and still others develop closed-mindedness towards it. Therefore such qualities of the object are merely created by preconceptions, and these preconceptions also do not exist inherently because they develop from superimposition.

[61] Whatever may be an object of examination does not exist inherently. As that object of examination does not exist inherently, how can the thought-consciousness of that non-inherently existing object exist inherently? Therefore, because the object of examination and the thought-consciousness arise from causes and conditions, they are empty of inherent existence.

[62] The mind which directly understands emptiness is an unmistaken mind which eliminates the ignorance that arises from the four evil preconceptions. Without that ignorance the karmic formations will not arise, and so neither will the remaining limbs.

[63] Anything which arises in dependence on any causes will not arise without those causes. Hence, functional

things in the form of produced phenomena and non-functional things as unproduced phenomena would be empty of inherent existence which is the natural state of nirvāṇa.

[64] The Teacher, Buddha, said that the conception of true existence of functional things which arise from causes and conditions is ignorance. From this ignorance arise the twelve dependent limbs.

[65] Understanding the non-inherent existence of things means seeing the reality [i.e., emptiness] which eliminates ignorance about the reality of things. This brings about the cessation of ignorantly grasping at an apparently true existence. From that the twelve limbs of dependent origination cease.

[66] Produced phenomena are similar to a village of gandharvas, an illusion, a hair net in the eyes, foam, a bubble, an emanation, a dream, and a circle of light produced by a whirling firebrand.

[67] There is nothing which exists inherently. In that fashion even non-functional things do not exist. Therefore, functional things which arise from causes and conditions as well as non-functional things are empty of inherent existence.

[68] Because all things are empty of inherent existence the Peerless Tathāgata has shown the emptiness of inherent existence of dependent arising as the reality of all things.

[69] Ultimate reality is contained within the limit of the non-inherent existence of a thing. For that reason, the Accomplished Buddha, the Subduer, has imputed various terms in the manner of the world through comparison.

[70] What is shown conventionally to the v .'ld appears to be without disintegration, but the Buddha has never actually shown anything with true existence. Those who do not understand what is explained by the Tathāgata to be conventionally existent and empty of the sign of true existence are frightened by this teaching.

[71] It is known in the way of the world that "this arises in dependence on that." Such statements are not refuted. But whatsoever arises dependently does not exist inherently, and how can that non-inherent existence itself have inherent existence? In fact, that non-inherent existence must definitely not exist inherently!

[72] Those who have faith in the teaching of emptiness will strive for it through a number of different kinds of reasoning. Whatever they have understood about it in terms of non-inherent existence, they clarify this for others, which helps others to attain nirvāṇa by abandoning grasping at the apparently true existence of cyclic existence and non-cyclic existence.

[73] By seeing these internal and external phenomena arising from causes and conditions they will eliminate the whole network of wrong views. With the elimination of wrong views they will have abandoned attachment, closed-mindedness and hatred and thereby attain nirvāṇa unstained by wrong views.

These Seventy Stanzas Explaining How Phenomena Are Empty of Inherent Existence have been written by the Teacher Ārya Nāgārjuna and complied by an unknown editor who referred to the better wordings and meanings of the translations by the translators Gzhon nu mchog, Gnyan dharma grags and Khu.

Section 2-2 Seventy Stanzas on Emptiness *with Tibetan Text and Commentary by Geshe Sonam Rinchen*

Sanskrit: *Shūnyatāsaptatikārikānāma*

Tibetan: *sTong pa nyid bdun cu pa'i tshig le'ur byas pa zhes bya ba*

Author: Nāgārjuna (kLu sgrub)

Text based upon the Peking Edition (P) #5227 (dbu ma tsa 27a-30b) printed in the Tokyo-Kyoto reprint of the bsTan 'gyur, D.T. Suzuki, Ed. and the sDe dge Edition (D) #3827 (dbu ma tsa 24a-27a) kept in the library of the University of California, Berkeley. Amended with reference to Candrakīrti's *Shūnyatāsaptativṛtti, sTong pa nyid bdun cu pa'i 'grel pa*, Peking Edition #5268 (mdo 'grel ya 305b-381b) printed in the Tokyo-Kyoto reprint of the bsTan 'gyur, and the sDe dge Edition kept in the Library of Tibetan Works and Archives, Dharamsala, India.

THE TITLE

rgya gar skad du/
sha'u naya ta' 1)sapta ti ka' ri 2)ka' na' ma/
bod skad du/
stong pa nyid bdun cu pa'i tshig le'ur byas pa zhes
bya ba/

1)D:sa pta 2)P omits ka' na'

SEVENTY STANZAS EXPLAINING HOW
PHENOMENA ARE *EMPTY* OF INHERENT
EXISTENCE.

THE SALUTATION

'jam dpal gzhon nur gyur pa la phyag 'tshal lo/

Prostration is made *to the Youthful Manjushri.*

When the translators of the past were translating texts
dealing with the training in higher wisdom they made pros-
trations to the Youthful Manjushrī in order to be able to
complete their work successfully. He is about sixteen years
old and remains in this youthful state forever because of his
high wisdom. All texts dealing with higher wisdom are
classified in the Abhidharma Piṭaka.

STANZA 1

/gnas pa'm skye 'jig yod med dam/
/dman pa'm mnyam dang khyad par can/
/sangs rgyas 'jig rten snyad dbang gis/
/gsung gi yang dag dbang gis min/

"Arising," "enduring," and *"disintegrating;" "existing"* and *"non-existing;" "inferior," "middling,"*
and *"superior" do not have true* existence. These
terms are used *by the Buddha in accordance with
worldly conventions.*

The Buddha has abandoned both the obscurations which
prevent liberation and the obscurations which prevent
omniscience. Thus he can perceive in a single instant both

the absolute truth about phenomena and the conventional truth of how phenomena appear to ordinary people. Although Nāgārjuna himself outwardly appeared to ordinary people to be a first stage Bodhisattva, inwardly he was actually a Buddha.

The term "arising" refers to a situation in which some phenomenon like an object or a thing is caused by some other phenomenon. By this it is meant that certain causes and conditions have the power to bring about the arising of a phenomenon, for no phenomenon can arise by its own power. But this does not mean to imply that the presence of some god, such as Shiva, is necessary for the arising of something.

When we carefully examine a phenomenon we find that the basis of its presumed existing as an independent entity is unfindable, and yet the phenomenon does arise in dependence on certain causes and conditions. We also find that all phenomena come into existence with imputation. By this is meant that we impute certain characteristics upon a basis of imputation (which basis is actually unfindable upon analysis) and the basis of imputation and the imputed phenomenon should be recognized as merely dependently arising phenomena. The concept that "there is a thing or phenomenon which arises without imputation" is to be abandoned through meditative analysis and it is Nāgārjuna's purpose in this treatise to refute erroneous conceptions about phenomena.

Such phenomena as arising, enduring and disintegrating, and also the terms "arising, enduring, disintegrating" do not have true existence. This does not mean that they are totally devoid of any kind of existence, but that they are devoid of inherent existence. True existence refers to that which exists inherently from its own side without depending on any other thing. However, no phenomenon is dependent on itself for its existence, but all phenomena are dependent on other causes and conditions for their existence, so it is said that they are devoid of inherent existence or true existence or self-existence, which are synonymous in this context. It is not said that they are devoid of conventional existence, which is how they appear to the ordinary person, for they do appear before us in some fashion.

When it is understood that arising, enduring and disintegrating are devoid of true existence, then it will be understood that "existing" and "non-existing" are also devoid of true existence. Here "existing" is a term which refers to the aggregates, elements, entrances and composite phenomena of the present. "Non-existing" is a term which refers to the aggregates, elements and entrances of the past and future and to non-composite phenomena in general. These all are devoid of inherent existence because they all arise, endure and disintegrate. Likewise, "existing" and "non-existing" must be devoid of true existence because they are designated upon phenomena which are devoid of true existence such as the elements, etc.

"Existing" is also used to refer to the person, which is merely the "I" which is imputed on the collection of five aggregates. "Non-existing" refers to the non-person, which is the collection of five aggregates which serves as the basis for the imputation "I."

"Existing" can also refer to functional things and "non-existing" can refer to non-functional things. These too are devoid of inherent existence.

"Inferior" refers to deluded (i.e., non-virtuous) phenomena, "middling" refers to phenomena which are not specified as virtuous or non-virtuous, and "superior" refers to virtuous phenomena.

All these differing terms which are defined above refer to what lacks true existence, and are not used for what lacks conventional existence. They are used to eliminate the belief in inherent existence and to establish the belief in non-inherent existence.

STANZA 2

In the preceeding explanation it was said that "existing" is used in reference to the "I" which is imputed on the collection of the five aggregates, but that the "I" is actually devoid of true existence. Now someone may ask why it was, then, that Buddha spoke of the existence of a self or an "I" in many scriptures? The following stanza answers this question.

/dbag 1)med bdag med min bdag dang/
/dbag med min pas 2)brjod 'ga' med/
/brjod bya mya ngan 'das dang 3)mtshungs/
/dngos po kun gyi rang bzhin stong/
    1)P:med 2)P:brjod 'ga' 'ng med 3)P:mcu ngas

All phenomena must have either *self-existence* or *non-self-existence*. There *is no* phenomenon which is other than these two, *nor are* there *any expressions* which do not come under these two catagories. *All phenomena* which are the *subject* of this treatise are *similar to nirvāṇa* because *all phenomena are devoid of 4)inherent existence.*
    4)rang bzhin

It is not possible to talk about phenomena, such as the "I," without using the two catagories of self-existence and non-self-existence, although in actuality all phenomena are devoid of self-existence. In order to recognize the grasping at self which is to be eliminated one needs to know the distinction between the "conventional I" and the "I" or "self" which is to be refuted. Buddha speaks about an "I" in order to refute it's self-existence. Considering the "I" or "self" which is to be refuted he said there is "no I or self." But considering the "conventional I or self" he said there is "I or self." Because he has seen the non-existence of the "I" which is refuted he taught us that it is the "conventional I" who performs actions, roams in cyclic existence, attains liberation and the state of Supreme Enlightenment.

Nirvāṇa refers to a state which is beyond suffering. Grasping at self (which is the object of elimination), arises when a person focuses on the "conventional I." When he is introduced to the "emptiness of self," then a good acquaintance can be gained through meditation on it, and after meditation he can see it directly. The practice of meditation will help him to see the exhaustion of the grasping at self-existence of self with its seed. That is, the non-inherent existence of an I is seen when its inherent existence is refuted. Then one can abandon the grasping at self by meditating on what one has seen — the emptiness of inherent existence of an I. At this point, the person attains the state of nirvāṇa and becomes an Arhat. From the time he becomes an Arhat he will never take rebirths through actions and grasping at self-existence of self, the object of elimination. When a person refutes the inherent existence of phenomena what remains is their conventional existence, and this is similar to the state of intrinsic liberation (rang bzhin myang 'das). According to the Prāsaṅgika Mādhyamika school one attains the state of nirvāṇa without remainder before attaining the state of nirvāṇa with remainder. But Svātantrika Mādhyamika and the schools below assert that a person attains the state of nirvāṇa with remainder before the accomplishment of the state of nirvāṇa without remainder.

STANZA 3

As there are different views about inherent existence, some persons may still not understand how the various phenomena and nirvāṇa are similar in the aspect of their being empty. Therefore, the following stanza is put forth to answer some objections which they may raise.

> /gang phyir dngos rnams thams cad kyi/
> /rang bzhin rgyu 1)rkyen tshogs pa 'm/
> /so 2)so'i dngos po thams cad la/
> /yod min de 3)phyir stong pa yin/
>   1)P:rkyin 2)P:so 3)P:pyir

What is the reason for this? It is because the *inherent existence of all phenomena* is not to be found in

causes, conditions, aggregations or individualities.
Thus all phenomena are devoid of inherent *existence*
and *are empty.*

What is the reason that phenomena are devoid of inherent existence? It is because there is no phenomenon which arises without depending on causes, conditions and the aggregation of causes and conditions. "Cause" means immediate cause and "condition" means contributing condition. "Aggregation" refers to these being joined together and "individuality" means taking them separately. For example, in the case of a phenomenon such as a sprout, a seed is the immediate cause of the sprout while water and earth are contributing conditions which allow that cause to come to fruition, or produce a result, which is the sprout. Also, contributing conditions produce general classes of results while causes produce specific results. In the case of the example above, water can contribute to the production of any sprout, but a specific seed is the cause for a specific sprout. If we examine causes, conditions, and their aggregations we discover that their individual existence is unfindable because they can not be separated and still retain their own natures in dependence on each other. In our example, if water is examined separately from the sprout, earth and seed we can hardly call it a condition which exists with the nature of a condition independently of the other factors, for without taking the result, the cause and the other conditions into consideration at the same time as one considers the water, that water is not a condition for anything. All these phenomena are interdependent, and since only an independent phenomenon could have inherent existence, which is existence by its own nature alone, so no phenomenon has inherent existence and all phenomena are empty.

STANZA 4

/yod phyir yod pa skye min te/

/med phyir med 1)pa skye ma yin/
/chos mi mthun 2)phyir yod med min/
/skye ba med pas gnas 'gag med/
   1)P:pas 2)D:pyir

Some assert that a result already *exists* inherently in
the nature of its cause; but then it *cannot arise
because* it already *exists*. Others assert that a result
exists inherently but *not* in the nature of its cause; so
it *cannot arise because* it *is not* in the nature of its
cause. Yet others assert that a result both does and
does not exist inherently in its cause; but then they
are asserting *contradictory* views about an *object because* an object *cannot* simultaneously both *exist* and
not exist. Because phenomena *do not arise* inherently
so also they *do not endure* or *cease* inherently.

Some persons assert that there are individualities or individual things which have an existence which is independent
of causes and conditions and that upon examination such
independence can be found. They say that results have the
same nature as their causes and that during the time of the
existence of a cause, its result exists in the cause in the form
of a potential which bears the same nature as the cause.
Since the result exists within the cause at the time of the
cause, they assert that the cause and the result must have
the same nature, and that they are inherently existent. As
their existence is thus not dependent on anything which is
other than themselves, so they exist independently as individual things. We refute that assertion by saying that if a
result were inherent in the nature of its cause then because
it would already exist in the cause at that time there would
be no need for the result to arise from the cause at some
future time.
   Some others respond to our refutation by asserting that
even if the result is not inherent in the nature of its cause,
still it does have an inherent existence which is independent
of its cause. But we refute this because all results depend on

causes, so how can they have independent, inherent existence? Any result which is asserted to be independent of a cause must be completely non-existent; like the horns of a rabbit, it is impossible for such a result to arise.

A third kind of assertion is made by some which is a combination of the first two. They say that although a result does not exist in the nature of its cause as an entity, still it does exist as a potential. But this is also incorrect because they are asserting the simultaneous existence and non-existence of a phenomenon before the time of its arising. It is not possible for a single phenomenon to simultaneously have two contradictory states of existence.

For example, some people assert that a vase has two aspects: one aspect is the form of the vase which appears before our eyes, and the other aspect is the aggregation of the elements which we discover when we closely examine the vase. They say that the vase does not exist as an entity, but that it does exist as a term "vase" which is imputed on an aggregation of elements which actually exist. We say that the term vase is imputed on an aggregation of elements, but that if we were to examine those elements we would see that they are as unfindable as the vase; thus there is no contradiction in our assertions. But their assertions are contradictory because they assert the existence of one aspect of a phenomenon and the non-existence of the other.

Now these refutations may lead to some confusion about the occurrence of phenomena such as the person, and a question may be raised, does the person endure or not? We say that the person endures, but not inherently, because a person is a phenomenon which is produced and is compounded. Produced and compounded phenomena do not have inherent existence, but they do exist conventionally as produced and compounded phenomena. In this manner they do arise, endure, disintegrate and cease and it is in this manner that when a phenomenon has newly arisen we say "the arising of a thing," "the enduring of a thing," and so forth.

STANZA 5

Some people have the view that the composite things which arise, endure and disintegrate do have inherent existence. The following stanza refutes this view by showing its contradictions.

/gang zhig skyes de bskyed bya min/
/ma skyes pa yang bskyed bya min/
/1)skyes 2)pa dang ni ma skyes 3)ba'i/
/skye bzhin pa yang bskyed bya min/
  1)P:skyed 2)P,D:ba 3)P,D:pa'i

Whatsoever has already *arisen will not* be able to *arise*. Whatsoever has *not arisen will not arise*. Either a phenomenon has already *arisen or* else it *will arise;* there is no other possibility beyond these two. Whatever is in the *process of arising* should 4)have already arisen or else it will arise in the future.
  4)Lit: bskyed bya min; is no future arising.

A produced phenomenon, as we have already shown, does arise, but it does not arise with inherent existence. If it had inherent existence then it would be independent, so causes and conditions could not produce it and thus it could not arise.

Now, a phenomenon must exist in either the past, present or future. If it is said that some phenomenon with inherent existence had somehow been produced on some occasion in the past, then it could not be produced again on some future occasion because of its already having been produced. And if it is said that it could somehow be produced again then it would never become something not to be produced and so would never cease being reproduced. Thus it is said that whatever has not arisen will not arise.

A phenomenon which has not yet arisen cannot be apprehended because it does not yet exist, so any statements which are made about it are meaningless. Thus it is not possible to assert that certain things can act as its causes and conditions, for this would be to assert that a non-existent phenomenon has causes and conditions. Moreover, such a non-existent phenomenon cannot provide a basis on which the activity of production could take place, so how could it ever be produced by causes and conditions? Thus it is said that whatever has not already arisen will not arise in the future.

There are no other possibilities for phenomena beyond their having already arisen or having not yet arisen. If it is asserted as an alternative that a phenomenon with inherent existence is currently in the process of arising, then that phenomenon is being asserted to be partly arisen and partly non-arisen. The arisen portion must have arisen in the past, while the non-arisen portion would have to arise in the future. But it has already been shown that anything with inherent existence which has not yet arisen will not be able to arise in the present or the future because it has no basis on which causal activity can take place and that anything with inherent existence which has already arisen will not be able to arise again in either the present or the future. Therefore a phenomenon with inherent existence cannot be partly arisen and partly non-arisen, and so such a phenomenon cannot be currently arising.

What is being refuted here is the inherent existence of a presently arising phenomenon, not its conventional existence, which appears before one. For example, take the case of a green shoot which is asserted to have inherent existence and to be currently arising. Such a green shoot cannot be shown to arise from a cause because the shoot must have either already arisen or not arisen; it has already been demonstrated that there is no third case. If it is said that it has already arisen, then it can't be said that it is currently arising for that is contradictory. Nor can it be said that it has not yet arisen and will arise in the future because it is appearing before one in the present. Thus it is clear that a presently arising phenomenon with inherent existence is unfindable and the belief in such a phenomenon is based on fallacies and contradictions.

STANZA 6

/'bras bu yod 1)par 'bras ldan rgyu/
2)/med de 3)la yang 4)rgyu min mtshungs/
/yod min med pa'ng min na 'gal/
/dus gsum rnams su 'thad ma yin/
    1)P,D:pas 2)P and D interpolate an extra line
    here which is not found in Candrakīrti; it reads
    /rgyu min dang mtshungs med pa *yang/ (*P:pa'ng
    for D:yang). 3)P:la'ng 4)P:rgyun

The *cause of a result* which already *exists* is similar to
that which *is not* a cause. *Also* in the case where a
result does not already exist, then its cause will be
similar to that which *is not a cause.* A phenomenon
should be either existent or non-existent but cannot
be *both non-existent* and *not-non-existent* because
these two are *contradictory.* Therefore it *is not suitable* to assert that there is either an inherently existing cause or an inherently existing result *in the
three times.*

The arguments which were previously applied to results
can also be applied to causes and cause-effect relationships,
demonstrating that they too lack inherent existence. The
relationship between cause and effect can be sought in the
past, the present or the future. Furthermore, in regards to
that relationship, if there were a result with inherent existence, then that result should have been produced by a cause
with inherent existence.

If the relationship is asserted to exist in the past, then a
result with inherent existence must have existed in a potential form at the time of its cause. We have already refuted
this possibility when we examined results. Also, if we examine the cause, we find there is no need for a cause for the
production of that result, for it already exists, so what is
asserted to be a cause of a result does not have the characteristics of a cause and is similar to that which is not a cause.

If a result does not currently exist and it and the causal relationship with it are in the future, then how can something be identified as causing it? Such a thing cannot act as a cause because no result exists. For example, yogurt is made from milk, not water. But without there being any yogurt we cannot say that this milk is a cause of yogurt whereas this water isn't, because neither of them have causal properties in relation to some result for there is not yet any result to which they can be related as having causal properties.

If it is said that the cause and effect relationship exists in the present, then both the cause and the effect must exist in the present. But this is contradictory and destroys the relation between cause and effect. For example, if it is said that a seed is the cause of a shoot with inherent existence in the present, then that seed must also have inherent existence, and then both seed and shoot would have to exist simultaneously, as things with inherent existence do not perish. But if they exist simultaneously, then no cause and effect relationship can be asserted between them.

Thus no inherent existence can be found in the relationship of cause and effect in any of the three times.

STANZA 7

Now, when some persons hear that it is not possible to assert the inherent existence of causes in the three times, they might wonder how this is possible because causes are numerous in number, so they should exist inherently. These persons further argue that it is not possible to refute the existence of causes because Buddha has enumerated many causes. Thus the causes must exist inherently because if they did not exist inherently how could Buddha have made enumerations of so many causes? For example, they say, how can we count the number of hairs on the back of a tortoise when there aren't any hairs on the back of a tortoise? Nāgārjuna refutes this argument in the following stanza.

/gcig med 1)par ni mang 2)po dang/
/mang po med par gcig mi 'jug/
/de phyir rten cing 'brel 'byung ba'i/
/dngos po mtshan ma med pa yin/
   1)P,D:bar 2)D:go

Without one there cannot be *many and without many*
it is *not possible* to refer to *one. Therefore* one and
many *arise dependently* and such *phenomena do not
have* the *sign* of inherent existence.

We refute their argument because the making of enumerations actually shows that causes do not have inherent
existence. This is because when we enumerate many things
we must first start counting with "one," and then we can go
on to count the "many." Because we must first have a
"one" before we can have a "many" so the "many" are
dependent on the "one." Likewise, we cannot find a "one"
without contrasting it with "many." Thus one and many
arise interdependently, and neither can be found to exist
without the other. Since it is the case that the many arise in
dependence on the one, so the Buddha's enumerating many
causes demonstrates that causes arise in dependence, and as
they arise in dependence, so they lack the sign of inherent
existence, which is independence.

The word "sign" (mtshan ma) has somewhat different
meanings in different contexts. In some cases it refers to the
aspects of phenomena, in other cases it refers to inherent
existence and sometimes it refers to reasons. For example,
the idea that all things have inherent existence is baseless
and without reason. Here we say that they lack the sign of
inherent existence and signlessness refers to the reason
which is lacking inherent existence. Sometimes sign refers
to the conventional mind. For example, if we bring two
colors together such as yellow and blue, we say that they
have different aspects or that they have different signs. A
thing's sign allows us to differentiate that thing from
another thing. But this is only so for the conventional mind

which does not examine things in their ultimate nature. In the spirit of emptiness, which is the ultimate reality of things, we find that things lack different aspects, or that they have the same aspect, but to the conventional mind they have different aspects because that mind does not examine things in the spirit of emptiness.

"Sign" should not be confused with "mark" (mtshan nyid), which refers to the nature or identity or definition of a thing. A mark helps us understand a particular thing with our mind. For example, arising, enduring and disintegrating are the marks of composite things. These are the characteristics or the definition by which we understand that things are composite. When we do not find these marks, then we know that things are not composite.

STANZA 8

In the previous stanza the opponent's view of the enumeration of causes was refuted, and now he asserts that there should be causes with inherent existence because of the teaching of the twelve limbs of dependent origination. Nāgārjuna now refutes that assertion by showing how this argument is based on an overestimation or superimposition on the twelve limbs.

> /rten 'byung yan lag bcu gnyis gang/
> /sdug bsngal 1)'bras can de ma skyes/
> /sems gcig la yang mi 'thad cing/
> /du ma la yang 'thad ma yin/
>   1)P:bral

The *twelve limbs of dependent origination result* in *suffering:* since the twelve limbs and suffering *do not arise* independently of each other, they don't exist inherently. *Furthermore,* it *is not acceptable* to assert that the twelve limbs are based on a *single* moment of a *mind nor* on *successive* moments of a mind, as such moments arise dependently and do not exist inherently.

The twelve limbs start with ignorance and karmic formations and end with aging and death. They do produce
suffering, but the very fact that they produce suffering
proves that suffering is dependent on the twelve limbs. If
suffering is dependent on the twelve limbs then it does not
have a self-sufficient existence and so is without inherent
existence. Moreover, the twelve limbs are a cause only in
dependence on the production of the result of suffering, so
they too, as a cause, do not have inherent existence because
they are dependent on suffering.

Furthermore, the twelve limbs need a mind basis on
which their activity can occur. Such a mind basis must be
either a single moment of mind or a succession of moments
of mind, that is, a mind stream. It is not possible to assert
that in a single moment of mind all twelve limbs occur
simultaneously because that destroys the temporal cause
and effect relation between the limbs. It is also not possible
to assert that all twelve limbs occur simultaneously over
many moments of a mind stream because this would mean
that all twelve limbs and the mind stream would have a
simultaneous cause and effect relationship.

It is not possible to assert that in a single moment of mind
all twelve limbs occur sequentially because this destroys the
meaning of "a moment," nor is it possible to assert that all
twelve limbs occur simultaneously but over a sequence of
many moments of mind because this destroys the meaning
of "simultaneous."

Rather, both the twelve limbs and the mind basis must
occur either simultaneously or sequentially, but this also
cannot be used as an argument for the inherent existence of
the twelve limbs. We have already shown how they cannot
occur simultaneously but they also cannot occur sequentially and have inherent existence. This is because such an
argument would depend on either each moment of mind or
the successive moments of the mind stream having inherent
existence. But if each moment existed inherently we could
not find the successive moments because succession re-

quires that preceeding moments cease and this is contrary to the assertion of moments having inherent existence. But if there is no succession of moments with inherent existence so there can be no sequentiality for the moments and no sequential basis on which the twelve limbs can occur.

Therefore, there is no way to argue that the twelve limbs have inherent existence and so they can not be used as a basis for arguing that their causes have inherent existence.

STANZA 9

In the preceeding stanza we have said that ignorance (the first limb) cannot exist inherently, but some understand this to mean that it does not exist at all. They say that this is wrong and that ignorance does exist inherently as a result of the mind misapprehending objects in four distorted ways. Nāgārjuna agrees that an inherently existing ignorance could arise from the four distortions if they had inherent existence, but they don't, and he explains this below.

> /rtag min mi rtag min bdag dang/
> /bdag min gtsang min mi gtsang min/
> /bde min sdug bsngal ma yin te/
> /de phyir phyin ci log rnams med/

> Because contaminated things arise in dependence on one another they *do not exist* inherently as *permanent* phenomena nor *do they exist* inherently as *impermanent* phenomena; neither as phenomena *with self-nature nor without self-nature;* neither as *pure* nor *impure; neither* as *blissful nor* as *suffering. It is thus* that the four *distortions do not exist* as qualities which inhere in phenomena, but rather are imputed to phenomena.

The four distortions are four qualifications of composite and contaminated phenomena. The four distortions are the taking of impermanent phenomena as being permanent, impure phenomena as being pure, selfless phenomena as having self and suffering phenomena as being blissful. They are a misapprehension of an object through ignorantly over-estimating its nature and superimposing characteristics on it.

As it is often said that the root of ignorance is the mis-apprehension of self-existence in phenomena, and that many things arise out of this misapprehension, so one might ask if the distortion of taking selfless phenomena as having self is more fundamental than the other three distortions. This is not correct, however, for these four distortions are coarse misapprehensions, and one is not more fundamental than the others. The belief in the inherent existence of a self-nature in phenomena which is the root of ignorance is a subtle misapprehension.

Now, one might develop some understanding about the four distortions and thus conclude that if phenomena are not permanent, are not pure, are not blissful and have no self, that they must be inherently impermanent, impure, suffering and without self-nature. But this is also incorrect. Since phenomena arise in dependence on each other they lack inherent existence, and also lack inherently existing characteristics of their own; they only have those character-istics which are imputed to them from our side. For exam-ple, if one grasps at the contaminated aggregates as in-herently existing impermanent phenomena, this is a subtler distortion than grasping at the contaminated aggregates as inherently existing permanent phenomena. Because if one understands that aggregates do not exist inherently as im-permanent phenomena, in this case, one has to understand that the aggregates do not exist inherently. But if one understands that the aggregates are not inherently existing permanent phenomena, here one does not need to under-stand that the aggregates do not exist inherently. An undis-torted mind does not superimpose any properties on phe-nomena and recognizes that not even emptiness or selfless-ness arise from the side of phenomena but are superimposed on them or imputed to them from the side of the mind. The opponent's error is in believing that freeing the mind from the four distortions has revealed true character-istics which exist inherently and independently in the na-ture of phenomena. In a conventional sense it is true that phenomena are impermanent, etc., and thus in a conven-tional sense ignorance does arise from the four distortions. But actually, because all phenomena arise in dependence on other phenomena, they do not have inherent existence and so neither do the characteristics which are attributed to them. Whether these characteristics are the four distortions or their opposites, they all are superimposed characteristics and these characteristics are devoid of inherent existence in the nature of those base objects. And, therefore, the ignor-ance which conventionally arises from the four distortions must also lack inherent existence.

STANZA 10

/de med phyi ci log bzhi las/
/skyes pa'i ma rig 1)mi srid la/
/de med 'du 2)byed mi 'byung zhing/
/lhag ma rnams kyang de bzhin no/
   1)D:min grid las 2)D:byid

There are no four distortions which exist inherently *and thus* there *can be no ignorance arising from* them. *Because that* ignorance *does not exist* inherently it *cannot give birth to karmic formations, which means* karmic formations will not arise and *so also* the *remaining* limbs too.

If ignorance lacks inherent existence, then what is depen-dent on it must also lack inherent existence. Thus karmic formations, which arise in dependence on ignorance, must lack inherent existence as do the other ten limbs, each of which in successive order is dependent on the preceeding limbs.

There is a further problem with the opponent's position,

for actually he is unable to account for the existence of the four distortions. He believes that characteristics such as impermanence, selflessness, suffering and impurity have inherent existence in the nature of phenomena and that a mind which knows phenomena to have these characteristics is an unmistaken mind. For there to be an unmistaken mind there must be an opposite mind which is mistaken. If an unmistaken mind were to know phenomena to have inherently existing characteristics such as impermanence and selflessness, then a mistaken mind would know phenomena to have inherently existing characteristics such as permanence and self, etc., which are the four distortions. However, we argue that what the opponent calls an unmistaken mind is actually mistaken, for no characteristics exist inherently in the nature of phenomena, and a mind which believes them to exist inherently in the nature of phenomena is mistaken. Now if what the opponent calls an unmistaken mind is actually a mistaken mind, then what he calls a mistaken mind would be unmistaken, and he would be asserting that phenomena do have characteristics such as permanence and self. This is obviously incorrect. Thus both the mind which takes the four distortions to be inherently existing in the nature of phenomena and the mind which takes the opposite of the four distortions to be inherently existing in the nature of phenomena are mistaken and neither mind can be the basis for the arising of four distortions with inherent existence.

STANZA 11

/ma rig 'du byed med mi 'byung/
/de med 'du byed mi 'byung zhing/
/phan tshun rgyu phyir de 1)gnyis ni/
/rang bzhin gyis ni ma grub yin/
   1)P:nyid

Ignorance cannot originate as a cause *except* in dependence on the *karmic formations.* Also, the *karmic*

formations cannot originate except in dependence on
their cause, which is ignorance. *Because* ignorance
and karmic formations are *interrelated* as *cause* and
effect *so these two 2)are known by a valid cognizer not
to exist inherently.*
    2)ma grub yin

The adherents of the Vaibhāṣika school believe that
ignorance and karmic formations are secondary minds or
mental factors (sems 'byung) which simultaneously arise
from the main mind (sems). Because ignorance and karmic
formations simultaneously arise from the main mind, which
is their cause, so ignorance cannot arise without depending
on the simultaneous arising of karmic formations, and likewise karmic formations cannot arise without depending on
the simultaneous arising of ignorance. Since these two are
interdependent in this way, so each one is a cause for the
other one, which is its effect. As they are each the simultaneous cause and effect of the other, so they cannot have
inherent existence.
    This can also be known through another explanation. It
is clear how karmic formations are dependent on their
cause, which is ignorance, but ignorance, as a cause, is also
dependent on karmic formations. This is because karmic
formations result from ignorance, so ignorance is the cause
of karmic formations, and thus without depending on the
karmic formations we cannot say that ignorance is the cause
of those karmic formations. Therefore, because they each
have the relation of cause and effect to the other, so they are
not independent of each other and so they cannot have
inherent existence.
    An ordinary mind cannot come to an accurate conclusion
about this, but a valid cognizer, which is an unmistaken
mind investigating the ultimate nature of things, will not be
able to find any inherent existence in ignorance or karmic
formations.

STANZA 12

/gang zhig bdag nyid rang bzhin gyis/
/ma grub de gzhan ji ltar bskyed/
/de phyir gzhan las grub pa yis/
/rkyen gzhan dag ni skyed byed min/

By itself none of the twelve limbs can *originate inherently,* but must depend on the remaining limbs. *How then* can one limb *produce another* limb? Moreover, *because* one limb has *originated* as a cause in dependence on the *other* limbs, so how can it *act* as a *condition* for the *origination* of results such as the *other* limbs?

With the help of a valid cognizer we can understand how a thing doesn't exist inherently, and we say that such a thing "lacks inherent existence." Now, the view of the opponent, who has not developed such a valid cognizer, is that if ignorance, for example, doesn't exist inherently then it must be a non-existent thing. But since he has asserted that one limb produces another so he would then be asserting that a non-existent thing produces something. This would be like a son being born to a barren woman!

For example, how can the limb of ignorance, which does not exist inherently, produce the other remaining limbs? This ignorance has arisen as a cause in dependence on other factors such as karmic formations, etc., so how can that ignorance, which is not independent and has not arisen by itself, but is conditioned by those other factors, produce it's effects, which are the remaining limbs such as karmic formations, consciousness, etc.? Clearly, as ignorance does not have inherent existence, so it cannot produce the other limbs as effects with inherent existence. And obviously a non-existent thing cannot produce an existent thing, so the opponent's position is refuted in either case. But there are other limbs which lack inherent existence. The twelve limbs arise in dependence on each other, so they lack inherent existence, but they are not totally non-existent. Thus karmic formations, for example, arise in dependence on ignorance but do not arise inherently from ignorance. It is also like this with the rest of the limbs, from consciousness on to old age and death.

STANZA 13

We have said that cause and effect are interrelated because it is not possible to establish a cause without an effect. We say that they are dependent arisings in mutual relation. Now when the opponent hears this, he thinks that this means that cause and effect must exist simultaneously like a father and son. This is refuted in the following stanza.

> /pha ni bu min bu pha min/
> /de gnyis phan tshun med min la/
> /de gnyis cig 1)char yang min ltar/
> /yan lag bcu gnyis de bzhin no/
>   1)P:car

The *father is not* the *son* and the *son is not* the *father. These two* are *mutually not non-existent and the two* of them *cannot* arise *simultaneously.* It is *likewise* with the *twelve* dependent *limbs.*

A father is the cause of a son, so he is not that son. A son is the result of a father, so he is not that father. Thus it is established that the father is not the son and that the son is not the father. Because the father has produced the son, so he is called a father, but if he had not produced a son, then he could not be called a father. Now, both of them cannot arise simultaneously because then we could not establish a relationship of cause and effect between them. This would be like looking at the two horns on the head of a cow, which have arisen simultaneously, and saying that the right horn has caused the left horn.

The example of the father and the son is similar to the case of the twelve limbs of dependent origination; they have the same sort of relationship. Because they arise in dependence on each other they can't arise simultaneously, nor can they be mutually non-existent, nor can they arise without depending on each other, nor can they be nondifferent.

Now, one may wonder why we make this sort of argument, such as when we show how a cause can only arise in dependence on an effect. After all, we are not arguing that a particular cause is totally non-existent but rather that it can only exist as a cause in dependence on something else, in this case, a result. One might say that this is just arguing about definitions and terms such as "cause" and "effect." We say that there are differing levels of subtlety used in conveying the teaching of dependent arising. That which is produced in dependence on its causes and conditions is a coarse form of dependent arising. This law mostly applies to composite phenomena. But a phenomenon which is evolved in dependence on its parts and particles is a subtler form of dependent arising. This fact can be established on all phenomena. However, a phenomenon which comes into being merely through the imputation of those terms and concepts which are its designators is the subtlest form of dependent arising. It pervades each and every phenomenon.

All objects of knowledge can be analyzed in accordance with the reasoning which we are setting forth here, which shows how all things come into being in dependence on a basis of imputation and in dependence on terms and concepts. Thus, in order to understand how an object of knowledge, such as a thing, arises one must understand how an imputed phenomenon is imputed upon a basis of imputation. To understand this one must be able to separate the imputed phenomenon from the basis of imputation. For example, a person is merely imputed on his basis of imputation — the aggregates — but there is no person who does exist or evolve from the side of the aggregates which are his basis of imputation.

In the preceeding stanzas we have shown that all bases of imputation lack inherent existence and having established this we have also shown how terms and concepts lack inherent existence.

STANZA 14

In the preceeding stanza we talked about the lack of inherent existence and dependent arising, saying that dependent arisings do not exist inherently but do exist conventionally. In the next stanza this is shown through the use of a metaphor.

/ji ltar rmi 1)lam yul brten pa'i/
/bde sdug 2)de yi yul med pa/
/de bzhin gang zhig la brten 3)nas/
/gang zhig rten 'byung dang 'di 4)med/
   1)P,D:las 2)D:dang de'i yul 3)P,D:na 4)D:'d
   med

Just as in a *dream, happiness* and *suffering depend* on dream *objects* and upon awakening *these objects* are known *not to* actually *exist, likewise any* phenomenon which *arises in dependence on another dependent* phenomenon should be known *not to exist* in the manner of its appearance.

When we are dreaming, the various objects in our dreams and the feelings which arise in dependence on them seem real, but when we awaken we know that they were not actually there. For example, in a dream we may smell the odor of a flower garland worn by an attractive woman and derive some feelings of pleasure from the odor. If when we awaken we try to find out about the nature of the attractiveness of the woman in the dream and whether she really has an attractive nature we cannot find such a nature because in our waking state she is no longer there. When we are awake we know that the woman and the flower garland, etc., which appeared in the dream are devoid of being a real woman or a real flower garland. Likewise, all dependently arising phenomena do not exist in the way in which they appear to be; thus, they are false.

Similarly, when we see and examine the twelve dependent limbs we can come to understand that they do not exist inherently. For example, ignorance, which causes the arising of karmic formations, doesn't exist inherently and it doesn't give rise to karmic formations inherently. Therefore, the karmic formations have not arisen inherently from the cause of ignorance. It is just as with the objects in a dream: upon awakening it can be understood that they do not exist as they had appeared to exist during the dream. So we can come to understand that these limbs, such as ignorance, do not exist in the manner in which they appear to exist. This means that they do not exist inherently, which is how they appear to exist to the ordinary person, nor do any of the things upon which they depend. To return to our previous example, a woman in a dream does not exist as a real woman, although she appears to, but she does exist as a dream woman. Similarly, all dependent arisings do not exist inherently, as they appear to, but they do exist nominally.

STANZA 15

Taking dreams as an example, we have illustrated how all things do not exist inherently, but our opponent misunderstands the point of our example and makes the following statement.

/gal te dngos rnams rang bzhin gyis/
/med 1)na dman mnyam khyad 'phags dang/
/sna tshogs nyid ni mi 'grub cing/
/rgyu las kyang ni mngon 'grub min/
   1)D:dan man

Vaibhāṣika: *If* you assert that *phenomena don't exist inherently* then you are asserting that they don't exist at all. *So how* can you make distinctions like *inferior, middling* and *superior* or that there are *different* beings in the six realms of existence? *How then* can

you *assert* the *manifestation of a result* which arises
from causes?

Our opponent has misunderstood our example, and
thinking that when we say that phenomena don't actually
exist we mean that they don't exist at all, he accuses us of
nihilism. He says that if we assert that things don't exist,
then we can't make distinctions among those non-existent
things since those things are like a flower in the sky or the
horns on the head of a rabbit. Also, he says, we cannot say
that composite things arise from causes and conditions; yet
we can see how composite things do arise from causes and
conditions. For example, there are beings in the six realms
of existence, and we can see some of them, they manifest
before our eyes. But, he says, if things didn't exist then we
couldn't make distinctions such as the six realms, and there
could be no manifestation of results from causes, so there
would be no transmigration through the six realms. If manifest things such as persons or animals were not able to arise
from causes, then how would we account for the beings of
the six realms which we can see?

STANZA 16

We answer our opponent's charges in the following way.

> /rang bzhin grub 1)na rten 'byung gi/
> /dngos po med 2)'byung ma brten na/
> /rang bzhin med par ga la 'gyur/
> /dngos po yod dang dngos med kyang/
>   1)P:da 2)D:'gyur

Response: When you assert that *phenomena exist
inherently* you are asserting that *they do not originate
in dependence* on causes and conditions and thus that
phenomena actually do not exist. For *if* phenomena
do not depend on causes and conditions, then they
should have independent existence throughout the
three times. Therefore there *cannot be any inherent
existence* for *functional phenomena* which *arise* from

causes and conditions *or non-functional phenomena* which do not arise from causes and conditions, and there cannot be any third mode of existence for phenomena.

When the opponent asserts that phenomena exist inherently he is claiming that they have independent, self-sufficient existence, which means that such phenomena are not dependent on causes and conditions for their existence. Thus the opponent is stating that there are no dependently arising phenomena. But if phenomena do not arise dependently, then how can they ever cease to exist? So then they must exist over the three times. But this is clearly not the case because phenomena, such as beings, are not permanent. If they were permanent then they would be independent throughout the three times, but this would contradict the teaching of the manifestation of results from causes and of the transmigration of beings through the six realms (because the differing destinies of beings in the six realms and their alterations in form are the results of the accumulating of causes). Since such permanent unchanging phenomena are not to be observed, so phenomena must arise in dependence, which means that they are not self-sufficient and that they lack inherent existence.

This applies both to functional phenomena, which result from causes and conditions and are themselves the causes and conditions for other phenomena, as well as to non-functional phenomena, which do not result from causes or conditions and are themselves not the causes or conditions for other phenomena. There is no third alternative, so no phenomenon has an inherent existence and no non-existing phenomenon has an inherent lack of existence.

STANZA 17

/med la rang dngos gzhan dngos sam/
/dngos med 'gyur ba ga la zhig/
/de na rang dngos gzhan dngos dang/
/dngos med phyin ci log pa yin/

Opponent: *If* phenomena *do not exist* inherently, *how* can you use terms to refer to their *own* characteristics or their characteristics in relation to *other phenomena or non-functional phenomena?* Response: Although phenomena lack inherent existence, still we can use terms like *own*-characteristics, *other*-characteristics *and non-functional phenomena* for although these are unfindable upon analysis, still, like the objects of a dream they appear to have existence to ordinary perception. So the way they exist and the way they appear are different and these conventional *existences* are called *distortions* or false.

Now the opponent asks how can we even charaterize phenomena when they lack inherent existence? We answer that phenomena do appear to ordinary perception and so they can be characterized using various terms. This is similar to talking about the objects of a dream. Upon awakening they are known to be illusions and not to actually exist, yet we can use various terms to characterize them. So in regards to phenomena that lack inherent existence, we say that they have a conventional mode of existence which is how they appear to a nonanalytical mind but which is different than their actual mode of existence, and we refer to this conventional appearance as being false or distorted. Here the term "distortion" refers to the objects of perception, not the mind which is perceiving them.

These objects of perception are characterized in dependence on their own natures or other natures. For example, fire is not different than heat because fire has the nature of heat. So we say that fire has its own characteristics in dependence on heat. Now when we compare fire to water we find that it is quite different, that it has a different nature than water, so it has other characteristics than water. And water, as compared to fire, has other characteristics, but as compared to its own nature, it has its own characteristics.

STANZA 18

/gal te dngos po stong yin na/
/'gag pa med cing skye mi 'gyur/
/ngo bo nyid kyis stong pa la/
/gang la 'gag cing gang la skye/

Hīnayānist: *If phenomena are devoid* of inherent existence *then* they will be completely non-existent like the horns of a rabbit, and so there can be *no occurrence* of their *arising or* their *cessation.* As Buddha has spoken about *arising and cessation,* they must exist, so how can things be *devoid of* 1)*inherent existence?*

1)ngo bo nyid

This opponent has also misunderstood our teaching about phenomena being empty of true existence or inherent existence. He mistakenly believes that when we say that phenomena lack inherent existence we mean that they lack any existence at all and that our view is that phenomena are completely non-existent. So he asks how can a non-existent phenomenon arise or cease? He goes on to refute our view by asserting that arising and ceasing must exist because Buddha has used these terms. We answer in the next stanza.

STANZA 19

/dngos dan dngos med cig car med/
/dngos med med na dngos po 1)med/
/rtag tu dngos po'ng dnos med 'gyur/
/dngos med med par dngos mi srid/

1)P:min

Response: An object *cannot simultaneously* arise as a *functional phenomenon* and cease as a *non-functional phenomenon.* If a *non-functional phenomenon does not exist then* a *functional phenomenon cannot exist* because an object cannot *arise* and endure as a *functional phenomenon* without depending on its cessa-

tion as a *non-functional phenomenon,* or else it would
exist at all times. If a *non-functional phenomenon*
which is different from a functional phenomenon
does not exist then it *is impossible* for a *functional
phenomenon* to exist.

Functional phenomena are produced by causes and conditions, and are themselves the causes and conditions for
other phenomena. Non-functional phenomena are not produced by causes and conditions and are not themselves the
causes and conditions for other phenomena. Thus it would
be contradictory to say that a phenomenon can simultaneously arise as a functional phenomenon and cease as a
non-functional phenomenon. Rather, a phenomenon must
sequentially arise as a functional phenomenon and cease as a
non-functional phenomenon. For this to be the case, functional phenomena and non-functional phenomena must be
different and must exist in mutual dependence because if a
phenomenon does not arise as a functional phenomenon, it
could not have been produced by causes and conditions and
could not produce results. Yet, if it does not cease as a
non-functional phenomenon, it will never cease producing
results and will be permanent. Thus a functional phenomenon cannot exist without a non-functional phenomenon and a non-functional phenomenon cannot exist
without a functional phenomenon; they are mutually dependent, but different. Since they occur at different times,
they cannot arise simultaneously but must arise sequentially, and they must lack inherent existence. This is because
phenomena that exist inherently exist independently, so if
they had inherent existence and arose simultaneously, then
they would exist permanently at all times, which is impossible. If they had inherent, independent existence and arose
sequentially, then they would be two different things without relationship. Thus no phenomenon can have inherent
existence, but phenomena must arise and cease without
inherent existence, and so Buddha spoke of arising and
ceasing.

What do we mean by arising, enduring, disintegrating and ceasing? These refer to four characteristics of a composite thing. Arising or production means the fresh arising of an identity of a thing from causes and conditions. Enduring refers to the abiding of the former continuity of a thing. Disintegrating refers to that which does not abide in the second moment of the time of its formation. Ceasing refers to the initial moment of a thing changing into the subsequent moment of a thing. When the process of disintegration has reached completion and the initial moment of a thing has changed into the subsequent moment of a thing, then the thing has ceased; it has gone beyond the limit of the original moment.

STANZA 20

/dngos po med par dngos med min/
/rang las 1)min zhing gzhan las min/
/de lta bas na de med na/
/dngos po med cing dngos med 2)med/
  1)P,D:med 2)D:na

If there *is no* arising and enduring, which are *functional phenomena, then* there *can be no* disintegration or cessation, which are *non-functional phenomena;* so the latter would be completely non-existent. If a phenomenon were to exist inherently it must have arisen from its own nature or from some other nature, but it *cannot* arise *from its own* nature *and* because a phenomenon cannot have a different nature than its cause, so it *cannot* arise *from* some *other* nature which has inherent existence. *Because of that,* a functional phenomenon *cannot exist* inherently *and* because a *functional phenomenon cannot exist* inherently, so a *non-functional phenomenon cannot exist* inherently.

Functional phenomena and non-functional phenomena are mutually dependent on each other for their existence,

which means that they do exist conventionally. This is
because arising is the characteristic of functional phenomena, while complete disintegration and cessation are
the characteristics of non-functional phenomena. If a phenomenon didn't arise, how could it disintegrate completely
and cease? Thus, without functional phenomena, non-
functional phenomena would be completely non-existent.
Likewise, we have already shown how the existence of
functional phenomena is dependent on the existence of
non-functional phenomena; thus they are mutually dependent for their existence, and since they are not independent
so they cannot have inherent existence.

If someone were still to assert that a functional phenomenon could exist inherently, then we would have to
investigate whether it had arisen from its own nature or
from another nature. Nothing can arise out of itself, so no
phenomenon can arise from its own nature. However, no
phenomenon can have a nature which is different than its
cause, so it could not arise from some other nature which
had inherent existence. So in neither case can a functional
phenomenon exist inherently, and because non-functional
phenomena exist in dependence on functional phenomena,
so non-functional phenomena must also lack inherent existence.

STANZA 21

/yod pa nyid na rtag nyid dang/
/med na nges par chad nyid yin/
/dngos po yod na de gnyis 'gyur/
/de phyir dngos po khas blangs min/

If a phenomenon were *to exist* inherently it should
be *permanent. If* a phenomenon were *to* 1)*disintegrate
completely then* you *must accept* the *annihilationist
view. If* a *phenomenon* were *to exist* inherently it
would either exist permanently or else undergo
complete disintegration: *it* cannot *occur* in a way

which is different than these *two*. *Therefore* one *should not assert* that a *phenomenon* has inherent existence.

1)Lit: med; not exist.

Phenomena which exist inherently cannot undergo change. Thus, over the three times a phenomenon with inherent existence must either remain permanent or else be completely non-existent. These are the only two possibilities for an inherently existing phenomenon, because if it can't change it must either remain the same at all times, i.e., be permanent, or else have disintegrated completely, i.e., become completely non-existent. The former is the eternalist view and the latter is the annihilationist view. Since these logical consequents are both extreme views, one should not assert that phenomena have inherent existence.

If we perform this type of analysis through reasoning, we will come to understand that all phenomena lack inherent existence and with this understanding we will be able to eliminate the ignorance of grasping at the true existence of all things. The ignorance of grasping at the true, inherent existence of things is different than the ignorance of grasping at the two extreme views about things, which are the overestimation of the nature of a thing, i.e., that it exists permanently, or the underestimation of the nature of a thing, i.e., that it is completelly destroyed or doesn't even exist conventionally. The two extreme conceptions are not directly contradicted in their apprehension of the object by the mind which understands that the referent object of the ignorance of grasping at true existence does not exist. But if through meditation we familiarize ourselves with the mind which understands the lack of inherent existence of things, then we will later be able to eliminate the mind which grasps at those two extremes of overestimation and underestimation.

STANZA 22

The opponent makes his answer in the next stanza, arguing

that in his view about objects there is no danger of falling into the extreme views of eternalism or nihilism.

/rgyun 1)gyi phyir na 'di med de/
/rgyu 2)byin nas ni dngos po 3)'gag/
/sngar bzhin 'di yang ma grub cing/
/rgyun chad par yang thal bar 'gyur/
   1)D:gyis 2)D:pyin 3)P:'ga'

Opponent: *Because of continuity* there *is no* danger of the two extreme views. *Acting* as a *cause* of another causal phenomenon the original causal *phenomenon ceases to exist.* Reply: *As explained before,* the cause and the result, like a functional phenomenon and a non-functional phenomenon, cannot arise with inherent existence either simultaneously or sequentially. In your view their lack of inherent existence makes them *completely non-existent,* in which case you cannot assert their *continuity* or that of the *moments* between them. *Therefore* the *faults* of the two extremes *remain* in your view.

The opponent is asserting that one can find many moments of the existence of a thing and that a continuity is maintained over these moments of a thing. He argues that because a continuity is maintained, so the extremes are avoided. For example, in the case of a seed producing a shoot, a continuity of the first moment of a seed is maintained over the moments between the cause, the seed, and the result, the shoot. He explains that because the shoot in its turn can serve as the cause of something else in a moment subsequent to it, so a continuity of the initial moment of the seed is thus maintained. This is because when the subsequent moment of the shoot arises the initial moment of the seed has ceased, but since the seed has produced something, its continuity is maintained upon that. Thus there is a continuity maintained between cause and result and since the initial moment has ceased and then the subsequent moment has arisen, so permanence is not being asserted and there is no danger of eternalism. Also, the second moment will give rise to a third moment, so there is no danger of the extreme of nihilism because although the second moment does cease, a third moment does arise and a continuity is maintained.

We refute this argument in the following way. If a cause and a result existed inherently, as the opponent maintains, then there would be no connection between them. This is because inherently existing things would be permanent, so one could neither assert their sequential arising and cessation, nor could one assert their simultaneous arising, because if they arose simultaneously, then they would lose their cause and effect relationship. Since inherently existing causes and effects can neither arise simultaneously nor sequentially, so it is impossible to say that a continuity of a cause is maintained in a result. Moreover, if it were to be asserted that somehow an inherently existing cause were to disintegrate completely, then how could one find its continuity with a result, because it has become non-existent? Therefore, in your assertion the faults of the two extreme views cannot be avoided.

STANZA 23

/skye 'jig bstan phyir sangs rgyas kyi/
/lam bstan ma yin stong nyid phyir/
/'di dag phan tshun bzlog pa ru/
/mthong ba phyin ci log las yin/

Opponent: When *Buddha explained* the *path* to liberation he *spoke* about *arising* and *disintegration*, so they must have true *existence*. Response: It is true that Buddha spoke about arising and disintegration, but they *are devoid* of inherent existence. For that reason the way *they appear* and the way they exist are *dissimilar*, and they appear in a *deceptive* way to the world.

This statement of our opponent is incorrect because the way arising and disintegration appear to ordinary perception is distorted. Because we have distorted perceptions, so arising and disintegration appear to ordinary perception as if they had inherent existence, but actually they lack inherent existence. So just because the Buddha spoke about arising and disintegration, that does not mean that he spoke about their having inherent existence.

STANZA 24

/gal te skye 'gag med yin na/
/ci zhig 'gags pas mya ngan 'das/
/rang bzhin gyis ni skye med cing/
/'gag med gang de thar min nam/

Opponent: *If arising* and *disintegration do not exist* then suffering can not exist, *so what cessation will bring forth nirvāṇa?* But because nirvāṇa can be attained that means there is suffering which has inherent existence and therefore there is arising with inherent existence and disintegration with inherent existence. Response: Nirvāṇa refers to that state where suffering *does not arise with inherent existence* and *does not cease* with inherent existence. *Don't we call that* state the 1)naturally abiding nirvāṇa? Therefore arising and disintegration do not exist inherently.

1)Lit: thar; liberation.

Our opponent believes that arising and momentary disintegration ['gag as it is used here is the same as 'jig in stanza 1] have inherent existence and are impermanent, so they lead to suffering. He believes that when this suffering is eliminated and completely ceases ('gags) one attains the state of liberation. He argues that arising, disintegration, suffering and nirvāṇa must have inherent existence, because if arising and disintegration didn't have inherent existence, they would be completely non-existent, in which case there would be no suffering which could result from them. And without suffering there would be nothing to free oneself from and no nirvāṇa to be attained. But, he argues, because nirvāṇa can be attained, this proves that suffering, arising and disintegration all exist inherently.

Nāgārjuna responds that all composite things, such as suffering, disintegrate, but that does not mean that liberation is attained. It is asserted in the system of the Lower Vehicle that nirvāṇa or liberation means the extinction of suffering or its continuity through the application of antidotes; however, the nirvāṇa mentioned here at this point, according to Mahāyānists, is not the one that the Hīnayānists are asserting but it has reference to the extinction of the inherent production and cessation of phenomena. In other words, phenomena are empty of inherent production and cessation; this is naturally abiding nirvāna or intrinsic liberation.

Conventionally, suffering can be extinguished by the power of antidotes, but in an ultimate sense, it can not be extinguished. Prāsaṅgika Mādhyamikas assert that all composite phenomena are in the nature of the extinction of inherent existence. The emptiness of inherent existence of all phenomena is the naturally abiding nirvāṇa which can be seen directly by a person on the Path of Seeing. Thus the terms "naturally abiding nirvāṇa" and "emptiness" are synonymous. When through repeated meditation one acquaints oneself with this mental state and abandons all the delusions, then one attains the state of liberation according to the greater vehicle system.

STANZA 25

The opponent, however, does not accept our assertions about the state of liberation because he does not accept that arising and disintegration lack inherent existence. So Nāgārjuna continues to show the fallacies in his view.

/gal te 1)'gags las 2)mya ngan chad/

/gal te cig shos ltar na rtag/
/de phyir dngos dang dngos med dag/
/mya ngan 'das par 3)rung ma yin/
   1)D:'gag 2)P:myang 'das 3)P,D:ru ngam

You have accepted that the *extinction* of the continuation of suffering is *nirvāṇa*, in which case you have held an *annihilationist view*. And *if* you 4)modify your position and assert that nirvāṇa is a state where suffering has inherent existence and has not been extinguished, *then* you accept permanent suffering which even includes the state of nirvāṇa, which is an *eternalist view*. *Therefore* you cannot assert that nirvāṇa refers to a state where suffering is a *non-functional phenomenon* which has been extinguished *nor* can you assert that nirvāṇa refers to a state where suffering is a *functional phenomenon* which has not been extinguished. These two assertions *about nirvāṇa are not appropriate*. Therefore nirvāṇa refers to that state where suffering does not arise with inherent existence and does not cease with inherent existence.

   4)Lit: cig shos ltar na; in the other way.

In general, a mere extinction of the continuation of suffering is neither permanent nor impermanent; it has become absolutely non-existent, therefore, how can it be a nirvāṇa? In fact, it can not be a nirvāṇa. A view based on such an assertion is a nihilistic view. If suffering doesn't exist, what liberation can be achieved by meditating on paths?

If the opponent now sees that such a view is fallacious, and modifying his position, argues that sufferings exist inherently and are not extinguished, then there is a new fallacy. In his modified assertion, the opponent has stated a view which is at the extreme of eternalism for he is asserting that sufferings are functional phenomena with a permanent existence, which means that they must remain as suffering phenomena even in the state of liberation. This is contradictory because liberation is a state which is free from suffering. Such a view also implies that one could not hope to attain a state of liberation because there is no way to extinguish a permanent phenomenon. Moreover, such an assertion contradicts the Buddha's teaching that the cessation of suffering is the state of liberation.

In our system, we assert suffering as being free from inherent production and cessation, thus we do not have the faults of eternalism or nihilism. Suffering exists conventionally but not inherently; its emptiness is the naturally abiding nirvāṇa, a kind of nirvāṇa explained here.

STANZA 26

In the previous stanza Nāgārjuna has refuted the opponent's assertions that suffering exists permanently or that it ceases to exist and is without continuity. So the opponent now comes to the conclusion that cessation is something which is different from a functional thing (which is a composite phenomenon which gives rise to sufferings). Nāgārjuna now refutes that belief.

/gal te 'gog pa 'ga' gnas na/
/dngos po las gzhan de yod 'gyur/
/dngos po med phyir 'di med la/
/dngos po med phyir de las med/

If you assert a *cessation* that is *different than a functional phenomenon* then you are asserting a cessation which does not depend on a functional phenomenon and which exists inherently and *permanently.* Because we have *refuted* the inherent *existence* of a *functional phenomenon* and also the inherent existence of a *non-functional phenomenon* which depends *on* a functional phenomenon, *so here* a cessation cannot have independent existence and so it *cannot exist* inherently or permanently.

If the opponent asserts that cessation is different than a

functional phenomenon, then he is asserting that it is a phenomenon, and a phenomenon must be either functional or non-functional. We have shown that non-functional phenomena depend on functional phenomena, and vice versa but if the opponent asserts that cessation is different than a functional phenomenon, then such a cessation will be a phenomenon which does not depend on a functional phenomenon and does not arise and cease; that is, it will be permanent. And since it does not depend on a functional phenomenon, so it will also be independent, and being independent it will have inherent existence. However, we have already shown that it is impossible for a phenomenon to have inherent existence, or be independent or permanent inherently.

In a general way we do accept that cessation is a permanent phenomenon, but this should not be confused with the opponent's view about permanent phenomena. He asserts a cessation which exists inherently and differently from functional phenomena: so it should have independent existence and should exist permanently. We do accept a kind of permanence, but it is a permanence that does not depend on any conditions or factors and which lacks inherent existence. No doubt we accept cessation as an existent phenomenon, i.e., a phenomenon which is permanent and doesn't depend on causes and conditions, but not as inherently existent.

STANZA 27

The opponent now asserts that nirvāṇa must have inherent existence because it has a definition. Nāgārjuna refutes this assertion in the following way.

/mtshan gzhi las gzhan mtshan nyid las/
/mtshan gzhi grub par rang ma grub/
/phan tshun las kyang ma grub ste/
/ma grub ma grub sgrub byed min/

Without depending *on the defined* one cannot estab-

lish a definition and without considering the *definition* one cannot *establish the defined.* As they depend
on each other, they *have not arisen by themselves,* so
therefore the *defined* and the *definition* are devoid of
inherent existence and also they do not exist inherently *in a mutually dependent way,* so *none* of
them *can be used to establish* the inherent existence
of another one.

"Defined" refers to the resultant establishment and "definition" refers to the causal establishment of the identity of
a phenomenon. Thus they are mutually dependent on each
other which proves that neither the "defined" nor the "definition" exist inherently. Since these two arise in dependence on each other, they have not arisen on their own, and
so they are not independent and therefore cannot have
inherent existence. This is also proved in another way: if
something were to exist inherently then there would be no
need for it to depend on its characteristics or definition, but
since the defined arises in dependence on its definition so it
exists in dependence on its definition. This reasoning also
applies to the definition, for if it existed inherently then
there would be no need for it to depend on what it defines.

Now Nāgārjuna's argument convinces the opponent that
the defined and the definition (or the object and its characteristics) exist interdependently, but he still believes that
they exist inherently. This is refuted in the second half of
the stanza. If the defined existed inherently then it would
exist without depending on the definition, and likewise if
the definition existed inherently then it would exist without
depending on the defined. But since they are interdependent they must lack inherent existence. Also, their mutual
interdependence itself lacks inherent existence. This is so
because it cannot be asserted that things exist inherently in
a mutually interdependent way when the objects which are
mutually interdependent themselves lack inherent existence. For example, a characteristic or definition of an object

(such as impermanence) cannot arise with its own identity without depending on an object (which is defined as impermanent). This is because we know an object through the perception of its characteristics and we know the characteristics through perception of the object. This being understood, we can see how it is incorrect to use something which lacks inherent existence as a reason or as proof or as evidence for demonstrating that something else has inherent existence, and if neither of them separately has inherent existence how could they jointly be used as a basis for proof that they exist inherently in a mutually dependent way?

STANZA 28

/'dis ni rgyu dang 'bras bu dang/
/tshor dang tshor ba po 1)sogs dang/
/lta po 2)blta bya 3)sogs 4)ci'ng rung/
/de kun ma lus bshad pa yin/
  1)D:scogs 2)P:lta 3)D:scogs 4)P,D:ca'ng

Following the logic of *this* explanation of mutually dependent origination one cannot use the *cause* of a *result* to prove that the result has inherent existence because the cause of the result originates in dependence on the result and so is devoid of inherent existence. The same applies to *all* the pairs such as *feeling and the one who feels or seeing and the seer, and so forth*. Taking these as examples one should understand how *all* the pairs *are explained* as being devoid of inherent existence because they originate in mutual dependence.

Following the logic of the argument just given at the end of the explanation of the previous stanza we can see how causes and results lack inherent existence. For a thing to be called a cause of another thing, it needs to come into relationship with that specific other thing. For example, for a man to be a father, that man must have a child. Not any child will do, but there must be a specific child who exists in dependence on a specific father. On this basis, we can call a man a father. We say that a father is the cause of a child, yet because that man can only be called a father in dependence on the existence of that particular child, so we see how the existence of a father arises in dependence on the existence of a child. The same logic applies to the child, which can only arise as a child in dependence on the existence of a father.

The father and the child exemplify the situation for all causes and results. A thing can only become a cause in relation to the specific result which it produces, and a thing can only become a result in relation to the specific cause which produced it. Thus cause and result arise in mutual dependence. As the logic of the previous stanza demonstrates, this means that they must both lack inherent existence, and that although they both have arisen in a mutually dependent way we cannot say that they have inherent existence in a mutually dependent way, and also that we cannot say that the relationship of mutual dependence has inherent existence. Furthermore, because each member of the cause and effect pair lacks inherent existence, it cannot be used to prove the inherent existence of the other. Thus one cannot use the cause of a result as a means of proving that a result has inherent existence.

This argument applies to all mutually dependent pairs of phenomena. Just as a cause is regarded as the producer of a result which is its product, so feeling is the experience of the one who experiences and seeing is the experience of the one who sees. In this way, the one who sees or feels exists in mutual dependence on seeing or feeling, and seeing or feeling exist in mutual dependence on the one who sees or feels. All such pairs therefore lack inherent existence. Furthermore, following the logic which we have demonstrated, no one of them can be used to prove that another exists inherently.

STANZA 29

Because we have refuted the inherent existence of phenomena, the opponent thinks that phenomena don't exist, in which case the three times wouldn't exist. But, he argues, because the three times do exist, so functional phenomena must also exist. We agree that if the three times were existent then functional phenomena would exist, but the three times do not exist inherently.

> /gnas med phan tshun las grub dang/
> /'chol phyir rang nyid ma grub phyir/
> /dngos po med phyir dus gsum ni/
> /yod pa ma yin rtog pa tsam/

Time does not exist inherently because the three periods of time *do not* maintain *continuity* by themselves, but *are dependent on each other*. If the three times were to have inherent existence in a mutually dependent way, then we could not make distinctions between them, but *because* we can *make distinctions* so time *itself cannot be established* as having inherent existence. *Because* time does not have inherent existence, the *functional basis* on which the three times is imputed *cannot* have inherent *existence, so therefore* the *three times do not have inherent existence* and are merely imputed by *concepts*.

Time does not exist inherently because there is no cognizer which cognizes the inherent existence of time and also because there is no cognizer which cognizes its continuity. The opponent believes that such a cognizer exists because we understand how hours are formed into days and how days are formed into months; thus, he says, we cognize the continuity of time. However, this is conceptual, it is not a direct cognition of the gross flow or continuity of time, which is its apparently enduring nature. We cannot directly cognize the continuity of time, so how can we assert that time has continuity? Since we cannot assert any continuity of time, then how can we assert there is any actual time, so, following the argument in stanza 27, it is impossible to actually make divisions in time, such as past, present, and future, except by way of their mutual dependence. Without their depending on each other we cannot identify them, so therefore they lack inherent existence, as must a supposedly existing continuity of time which is derived from them, as well as the functional basis on which we impute the three periods of time. The three periods of time also cannot depend on themselves, rather, the three periods of time depend on each other.

If it were argued that the three periods of time existed inherently in a mutually dependent way, then they should be mutually dependent in all times. But then we could not make distinctions between them and they would be all entangled. For example, the past would exist in the present. Moreover, if the three times existed inherently in a mutually dependent way then they would always remain the same, and we could, for example, find the present and the future in the past. But if these two exist inseparably from the past in the past time, then we couldn't make distinctions in the three times. But we can make distinctions, so this is incorrect. Because of these fallacies the three periods of time cannot exist inherently in a mutually dependent way but are merely imputed by concepts on a functional basis and this also lacks inherent existence.

The functional basis on which time is imputed has the nature of time but lacks inherent existence. This functional basis is unknowable when analyzed ultimately but must have some sort of existence in order for us to impute the qualities of time on it. If we do not understand this and we ask the question, is this functional basis in the past, present or future, we cannot answer this question. For example, take the case of a vase. The three times can be known with reference to it. The past of a vase is its cause. The future of a vase is its result. The present of a vase is its having existence. But it is different when we talk about a future vase (i.e., a vase in the future) at the time of its cause: it will be in the present when its whole identity is accomplished and it will be in the past after its identity is lost.

STANZA 30

/gang phyir skye dang gnas dang 'jig
/'dus byas mtshan nyid 'di gsum med/
/de phyir 'dus byas nyid ma yin/
/'dus ma byas la'ng cung zad med/

Following the reasoning just given, *the three charac-teristics* of a *composite phenomenon* which are *arising, enduring and ceasing* are unfindable upon ultimate analysis even for you, so then a functional phe-nomenon which is characterized by these three attributes is also unfindable, in which case the func-tional basis of a composite phenomenon becomes unfindable. *So when* a *composite phenomenon cannot exist* inherently, how can a *non-composite phe-nomenon* which depends on a composite phe-nomenon *have* inherent *existence in the least.*

If you perform a careful analysis you will conclude that there is a basis upon which terms are imputed but that this basis cannot be found. If such a basis existed inherently it should be findable, but because it cannot be found, so it cannot exist inherently. If this reasoning is applied to com-posite phenomena, we realize that ultimately they are un-findable, so they must lack inherent existence. Therefore, non-composite phenomena, which depend on composite phenomena, must also be unfindable and lack inherent existence.

For example, space is a mere negation of obstruction and contact. It is a permanent phenomenon merely imputed by terms and concepts on its basis of imputation: clear in-termediate vacuity visible to the eyes, which is a composite thing. As they are mutually dependent on each other and cannot exist without the other, that means they are empty of inherent existence.

Furthermore, how can we establish non-composite phenomena without depending on composite phenomena? For example, by abandoning the objects of abandonment we can obtain cessation, which is a permanent phenomenon. So in this case, cessation, which is permanent and non-composite, is obtained in dependence on abandoning composite phenomena.

STANZA 31

Composite phenomena are said to disintegrate momentarily (that is, they disintegrate over a period of successive moments) and this entire process can be characterized as the arising, enduring and cessation or complete disintegration of a phenomenon. Now if a phenomenon is asserted to exist inherently, then certain fallacies will result when we carefully analyze any single moment in one of these three periods of time and attempt to find the characteristics which are said to inhere in that phenomenon.

/ma zhig mi 'jig zhig pa'ng min/
/gnas pa gnas pa ma yin te/
/mi gnas 1)pa yang gnas ma yin/
/skyes pa mi skye ma skyes min/
   1)P:la'ng

At the point of its complete *disintegration* does a phenomenon disintegrate which *has already disintegrated* or at that point does a phenomenon disintegrate which *has not yet disintegrated?* In the first case the process of disintegration is complete, so this cannot be accepted. In the second case it is free from the function of disintegration, so this cannot be accepted. The same applies to enduring and arising. If a phenomenon were to *endure* at that point when it has already endured then the process of enduring is complete and we can*not* say that it is *enduring* at that point. *And* a phenomenon which has *not endured* cannot be accepted as enduring at that point because it *is free from* the function of *enduring*. If a phenomenon were to arise at the point of arising which has already *arisen* then the process of *arising* is already complete, so this can*not* be accepted. And if a phenomenon were to arise at that point which has *not arisen* then that case is not acceptable, because it *is non*-existent.

STANZA 32

/'dus byas dang ni 'dus ma byas/
/du ma ma yin gcig ma yin/
/yod min med min yod med min/
/1)mtshams 'dir sna tshogs thams cad 'dus/
   1)P:mtshan

If we examine *composite phenomena and non-composite phenomena* then we can*not* find them as *one*, because then we cannot differentiate between these two types of phenomena, and we can*not* find them as *many*, because then these two would be completely unrelated. If a composite phenomenon is asserted 2)*to exist*, then it cannot arise because it is already existent and if it is asserted *not to exist*, then it cannot arise because it is non-existent. If it is asserted to be both *existent* and *non-existent*, this *is not* possible because such a state is contradictory. *Every different* type of phenomenon *is included within this criterion* of non-inherent existence.
   2)Lit: not non-existent.

It is the view of the opponent that composite phenomena and non-composite phenomena have inherent existence, but Nāgārjuna shows that if we examine these phenomena from the standpoint of their having inherent existence, then certain fallacies are found. Composite and non-composite phenomena must be either the same ("one") or different ("many"). But if our examination shows them to be the same, then we cannot differentiate between them. Yet, if our examination shows them to have inherent existence and to be different, then they will be completely unrelated, like a tree and a vase. But this is contradictory because composite and non-composite phenomena are known through their relation to each other and we cannot find a composite phenomenon with a self-sufficient existence which doesn't depend on non-composite phenomena.

If the opponent accepts our argument up to this point, he may still assert that composite phenomena, at any rate, have inherent existence. Therefore we ask: within the context of your belief in inherent existence, does a composite phenomenon arise which is already existent, or does a composite phenomenon arise which lacks existence, or does a composite phenomenon arise which is both existent and non-existent? If a composite phenomenon exists inherently, it would exist from the beginning, so it would have no need to arise. But if it doesn't exist inherently, then it couldn't come into existence because it would be non-existent forever. Nor is it possible for a phenomenon to be both existent and non-existent as these are contradictory assertions in relation to a single object.

Thus we have shown that all composite and non-composite phenomena lack inherent existence, and since composite phenomena are compounded of parts and particles, all these must also lack inherent existence.

STANZA 33

The opponent now offers reasons to prove that phenomena exist inherently.

/bcom ldan bla mas las gnas dang/
/las bdag las kyi 'bras bu dang/
/sems can rang gi las dang ni/
/las rnams chud mi 1)za bar gsungs/
  1)D:bra

Opponent: The *Peerless Subduer* has taught that

there is *continuity in* the flow of *actions. Likewise,* he
has taught about the *nature* of *actions* and their
results. He has also *taught* that the results of *actions*
performed by an *individual sentient being* must be
experienced by him *and* that whatever *actions* are
performed 2)are *certain to bear fruit.* For these four
reasons actions have inherent existence.

　　2)Lit: chud mi za bar, will not be wasted.

　　The opponent believes that because the Buddha spoke of
a continuity in the flow of actions, this means that these
actions endure and have inherent existence. Continuity in
the flow of actions is understood to mean, for example, that
whatever actions we perform to accumulate wealth will bear
some fruit in the future, even though at death the wealth we
have accumulated will have to be left behind. The opponent
believes that this teaching of the Buddha shows that such
actions must have the nature of inherent existence or else
they could not endure into the future. Furthermore, the
Buddha taught that there is certainty that the result of
actions will have to be experienced by the one who performed them. For example, if a person performs nonvirtuous actions and does not apply the four powerful antidotes but continues to perform nonvirtuous actions, then it
is certain that *that* person will experience bad consequences.
Since the Buddha has taught about actions in these ways,
the opponent takes this as a proof that actions must have
inherent existence.

STANZA 34

We agree with the opponent that Buddha taught about the
law of action and result, but we disagree with him in that we
believe that Buddha taught these things conventionally, but
not ultimately. So where the opponent understands the
Buddha's use of the term "existence" to mean inherent
existence, we understand the Buddha to mean conventional
existence. We point out that the Buddha taught that all

composite or produced phenomena are impermanent. He also said that impermanent phenomena lack inherent existence. Because all actions are impermanent phenomena, so they must be devoid of inherent existence. If they did exist inherently then they couldn't be impermanent phenomena because phenomena which exist inherently should not undergo change.

/las rnams rang bzhin med gsungs te/
/ma skyes gang de chud mi za/
/de las kyang ni bdag 'dzin skye/
/de bskyed 'dzin de'ng rnam rtog las/

Reply: Buddha *taught* that *actions do not exist inherently* and so they *cannot arise* inherently. Although actions do not exist inherently, they *will not be wasted* but it is certain that they will bear fruit. *From these* actions *arise* consciousness, name and form, and the rest of the limbs of dependent origination. *Conception of self* 1)*is generated* through focusing on the person who is merely imputed upon these dependent limbs. *Also, it arises from the preconception* which *takes* improper objects and overestimates them.

    1)Lit: skye, arises.

STANZA 35

/gal te las la rang bzhin yod/
/de 1)bskyed lus ni rtag par 'gyur/
/las kyang sdug bsngal rnam smin can/
/mi 'gyur de phyir bdag tu 'gyur/
    1)D:bskyes

If actions were to have inherent existence then they would not be impermanent but would have the nature of permanence, and then the *body* which *results* from *those* actions *would* also *be permanent.* If *actions* were to be 2)permanent then they could not

give rise to *suffering,* which is the *ripening* of actions.
If actions were *non-changing then* they *would have*
the *nature* of permanence and then they would have
self-existence. But then Buddha would not have
taught about the lack of self-nature.
   2)Lit: mi 'gyur, unchangeable.

There must be a correspondence between cause and result, which is why, for example, nonvirtuous actions give
rise to suffering. Following this principle, if the opponent
asserts that actions have inherent existence, then so must
their results. This means that the body, which is the result
of previous actions, would have to exist inherently.
Moreover, if actions existed inherently, then they would be
permanent, and so would their results, which means that
the body would be permanent. This is clearly false.
   Also, if actions were permanent they could not give rise
to suffering because permanent phenomena cannot give rise
to results. This is because permanent phenomena do not
change, but for there to be some arising there must be some
change. Thus, actions cannot be permanent, because actions do produce suffering.
   The Buddha taught that all composite phenomena are
impermanent, and whatever is impermanent has a suffering
nature. Because whatever has a suffering nature lacks self-
existence, so actions must lack a self-nature.

STANZA 36

In the previous stanza we proved that actions lack inherent
existence by demonstrating the fallacies which result from
such a view. Now, taking another reason, we will again
prove that actions lack inherent existence.

   /las ni rkyen skyes yod min zhing/
   /rkyen min las skyes cung zad 1)min/
   /'du byed rnams ni sgyu ma dang/
   /dri za'i grong khyer smig rgyu mtshungs/
      1)P,D:med

If actions were to exist at the time of conditions, those *actions could not arise* from those *conditions*. And if conditions do not have the potential to give rise to actions, then actions cannot arise from conditions because those conditions are similar to non-conditions. Because *actions cannot arise even slightly* from *non-conditions,* so therefore all *composite phenomena are like* an *illusion,* and a *gandharva town* and a *mirage,* and therefore they lack inherent existence.

If actions exist inherently, do they arise from causes and conditions or not? If we answer that actions arise from conditions, then we must ask whether actions arise at the time of conditions or not. If an action does arise at the time of its conditions, then there is no need for the conditions, because the action is already existent at that time. If it doesn't, then the conditions have ceased when the action arises, so the conditions cannot serve their function in giving rise to the action. In this case, it is like a non-condition. It is impossible for actions to arise from non-conditions. Hence they lack inherent existence. All composite phenomena are empty of inherent existence like illusions and mirages, etc.

Here we are showing that actions lack inherent existence, but this does not mean that they are completely non-existent. Rather, they are non-inherently existent, like illusions and mirages.

STANZA 37

/las ni nyon mongs rgyu mtshan can/
/nyon mongs 'du byed las bdag nyid/
/lus ni lus kyi rgyu mtshan can/
/gsum ka'ng ngo bo nyid kyis stong/

Actions are *caused* by *delusions.* Our body arises *from the nature* of *delusions* and *actions.* Because the *cause* of the *body* is *actions,* and actions arise from delusions, *so therefore these three are devoid of inherent existence.*

In the previous stanza we have seen that actions have non-inherent existence, a type of existence which is like a mirage. Now Nāgārjuna shows us that these non-inherently existing actions are caused by delusions, and that these two are, in their turn, the cause of the body. Because body exists in dependence on actions and actions exist in dependence on delusion and because we have already seen that actions lack inherent existence, so all these three lack inherent existence. This is because whatever exists in dependence on something must lack independent, inherent existence. Applying this principle to the relation of delusion and action, it can be seen that since action lacks inherent existence, so too must its cause, delusion.

STANZA 38

Our opponent says that actions are inherently existent because a person who is dominated by ignorance is the performer of unmeritorious actions and accumulates them. As he exists, actions exist to produce results which would be experienced by him.

> /las med na ni byed po med/
> /de gnyis med pas 'bras bu med/
> /de med nye bar spyod 1)po med/
> /de bas dngos po dben pa yin/
>   1)D:pa, P:bo

When *actions do not* have inherent *existence* there *will be no person to perform* actions. *Because both of them do not exist, results do not exist.* When *there are no* results there *will be no person to experience* those results physically and mentally. *Because of that* reason that actions do not exist inherently, so all *phenomena are devoid* of inherent existence.

Since actions are devoid of inherent existence there can

be no truly existent person to perform actions, but only an illusory, conventionally existent person (which is described in stanzas 40-42). The results of the actions of such an illusory person are also, still in a metaphoric sense, illusory; that is, they are devoid of inherent existence. As we have already seen, the body and the mind, which are interdependent, lack inherent existence, so there is no truely existent person having body or mind to experience the results of previous actions. But there is a conventionally existent person having body and mind which does experience the conventionally existent results of conventionally existent actions.

STANZA 39

/las ni stong par yang dag 1)par/
/shes na de nyid mthong ba'i phyir/
/las 2)mi 'byung ste de med na/
/las las 'byung gang mi 'byung ngo/
   1)D:pa'i 2)D:ni

If one *understands* how *actions are* 3)*devoid* of *inherent existence, then* he *sees* the *suchness* of actions. *When* he has seen suchness he will have eliminated ignorance and when there is no ignorance then the *actions* which are caused by ignorance *cannot arise* in him, *and so* 4)*the results of actions* such as consciousness and so forth up to aging and death *will not be* experienced by him. When consciousness ceases to exist the dependent limb of aging and death cannot occur; thus he will attain the state of liberation free from aging and death.

   3)Lit: yan dag; real or perfect. The real nature of actions is their being devoid of inherent existence. 4)Lit: las las 'byung gang; that which originates from actions.

Actions cannot arise without a cause, so when one has understood how actions are devoid of inherent existence and seen the suchness of actions, then meditating on it one can eliminate the ignorance of grasping at the inherent existence of actions and since this ignorance is the cause of contaminated actions, so then such actions cannot arise. When contaminated actions cannot arise then their results, such as consciousness and so forth up to aging and death, also cannot arise and in that case one has achieved liberation.

However, a person who achieves liberation does not become absolutely non-existent. In fact, such a person will take rebirths in dependence upon his uncontaminated actions and thereby work for others. As he has abandoned delusive obscurations he won't be influenced by them in his activities. Therefore, his actions become virtuous. Any other view would be nihilistic because if one could not perform actions after attaining the liberation which comes from destroying ignorance, then one couldn't work for the benefit of others.

Within the context of the twelve dependent limbs, the dependent limb of consciousness does not refer to consciousness in general but rather refers specifically to the sixth, mental consciousness (yid kyi rnams par shes pa), which is associated with the mind sense organ. This consciousness receives the imprints of virtuous and nonvirtuous actions and entering the womb of the mother is the source of the person who ages and eventually dies.

STANZAS 40-41

> /ji ltar bcom ldan de bzhin gshegs/
> /rdzu 'phrul gyis ni sprul pa sprul/
> /sprul pa de yis slar yang ni/
> /sprul pa gzhan zhig sprul gyur pa

> /de la de bzhin gshegs sprul stong/
> /sprul pas sprul pa smos ci dgos/
> /gnyis po ming tsam yod pa yang/
> /1)ci yang rung ste rtog pa tsam/
>   1)D:gang ci 'ng

Through his *miraculous powers, Tathāgata the Subduer emitted* an *emanation and that emanation emitted another emanation. As* the *emanation* emitted by the *Tathāgata is devoid* of inherent existence, *it is hardly necessary to say* that the emanation *emitted by the emanation* is also devoid of inherent existence. When we say that these two emanations do not exist inherently, that does not mean that they are completely non-existent but rather that *both of them*, just like actions and the one who performs actions, merely *exist through terms* because they are separated from the nature of inherent existence. 2)*They* do exist, but *merely through imputation by thought* in a deceptive way.

2)Lit: ci yang rung; all that are existent.

Stanzas 40 and 41 give examples whose meaning is given in stanza 42. Though they constitute two separate stanzas, the Tibetan tradition is to explain them both at the same time.

Though the stanzas end with the assertion "They do exist ...," this does not simply mean that only actions and the actor or the various emanations merely exist through imputation by thought, but that all phenomena merely exist through imputation by thought. This means that all phenomena which conventionally exist have a deceptive appearance.

It is possible to know the basis of imputation of phenomena. For example, the five aggregates are the basis for imputing the existence of a person, and these aggregates are knowable. A person doesn't exist inherently from the side of his aggregates because he becomes unfindable under ultimate analysis, but he does exist conventionally by way of mere imputation by terms and concepts. Likewise, what you are now looking at is the basis for imputing the term "book," and when you see that the book is not inherently existent from the side of its basis of imputation, you have understood its emptiness of inherent existence. Because the book exists merely through the imputation of words and concepts that is indicative of its conventional existence.

Thus it is said that the world which we see merely exists through words and concepts and that there is no other world which exists except that world which exists through words and concepts. However, the imputations can be removed and the six sense organs can know the basis of imputation as it actually is.

STANZA 42

/de bzhin byed po sprul dang mtshungs/
/las ni sprul pas sprul dang mtshungs/
/rang bzhin gyis stong gang cung zad/
/yod pa de dag 1)rtog pa tsam/
   1)P:ni

The person who performs actions is said to be *similar to* the *emanation* emitted by the *Tathāgata* because he is led by ignorance. And so his *actions are* said to be *similar to* the *emanation* emitted *by* the *emanation.* All of these *are devoid of inherent existence,* though *they do* have a *slight existence as mere* imputations supported by terms and *concepts.*

Without the Tathāgata there could be no existence of the Tathāgata's emanation. Similarly, both the person who performs actions and his actions cannot come into existence without there being the ignorance which leads that person. As both of the emanations, being dependent on the Tathāgata, lack inherent existence, so also do the person who performs actions and the actions which are performed lack inherent existence, for they depend on ignorance.

Though the person who performs actions and the actions which are performed lack inherent existence, they are said to "have a slight existence." The meaning here is that they have an existence through mere terms and concepts, that is, they exist conventionally. If this were not the case, then

Nāgārjuna would be arguing from a nihilistic extreme, asserting the actual non-existence of phenomena. (On this point, cf. stanza 44.)

STANZA 43

/gal te las kyi rang bzhin yod/
/myang 'das byed po las kyang med/
/gal te med na las bskyed pa/
/'bras bu sdug dang mi sdug med/

If actions were to have the nature of *inherent existence*, then they would be permanent. But if actions were permanent then they would not depend on a person, and if there *were no person to perform actions*, then actions would not exist. In that case, *nirvāṇa*, which is the state of cessation of delusions and actions, could not be attained. *If* actions *did not exist* through mere terms and concepts *then their ripening results* such as *happiness and suffering could not arise*.

If actions are inherently existent they should be permanent and unchanging phenomena. In that case, nirvāṇa, which refers to the state of extinguished contaminated actions and delusions, could not be achieved. Moreover, such actions would be causeless as they could not depend on a person led by ignorance as their cause. But this is not appropriate. Also, if actions exist inherently they cannot have imputed existence, which means that happy and suffering results will not arise from them. But this is not true, as we can see how happy and suffering results occur from virtuous and nonvirtuous actions. This clearly speaks to the fact that they exist merely through the imputation of terms and concepts. In other words, they exist conventionally.

STANZA 44

In this stanza Nāgārjuna clarifies the language he uses when discussing extreme views about existence which may be held by various opponents.

/yod ces pa 1)dang yod med ces/
/yod dang med ces de yang yod/
/sangs rgyas rnams kyi dgongs pa yis/
/gsungs pa 2)rtogs par 3)bla ma yin/
  1)D:yod med ces yod 2)P:rtog 3)P:sla

Whatever is *said by the Buddha* has the two truths as
its *chief underlying thought;* it *is* 4)*hard to understand*
and must be interpreted in this light. When the
Buddha *says "existence"* his chief underlying
thought is conventional existence; when he *says
"non-existence"* his chief underlying thought is non-
inherent existence; when he *says "existence-and-non-
existence"* his chief underlying thought is conventional-existence-and-non-inherent-existence as a
mere object of examination.

  4)Lit: rtogs par bla ma; not easily understood.

Nāgārjuna himself must use predicates such as "exists"
in his discourse, but, like the Buddha, he does so only for
the purpose of instructing the ignorant who need to develop
a mental (generic) image of emptiness. He himself maintains the correct view as his chief underlying thought. In
order to argue against the extreme of nihilism he uses the
term "exists," thereby establishing conventional existence.
Then, at the next level, he says "does not exist" in order to
argue against the extreme of permanence, thereby establishing non-inherent existence. Finally, he says "exists-and-
does-not-exist" to show the middle view which is free from
both of these extremes. This is his real goal, the demonstration that things are actually mere objects of examination
upon which we impute extreme views. With this realization
we cease grasping at the supposed true existence of objects.

  In regards to the topic under discussion, the nature of
actions, the Buddha has made what appear to be contradictory statements, even though his chief underlying thought
has remained the same. This is because although his audience consistently held the view that actions exist inherently,

at different times the Buddha wished to refute different errors connected with this view.

When the Buddha said that "actions exist" he meant that they exist conventionally, but not inherently. He knew that if he said that actions did not exist inherently his auditors would misunderstand him and take non-inherent existence to mean actual non-existence. To preserve them from this extreme nihilistic view which leads to the three lower realms he therefore said "actions exist."

At other times the Buddha told the same audience that "actions do not exist," by which he meant that they do not exist inherently. Here his purpose was to counter the eternalist extreme that actions exist inherently and thus permanently, for unless his auditors discarded this extreme view they could not become free of cyclic existence.

At yet other times the Buddha said that actions "exist and do not exist," by which he meant that actions exist conventionally and non-inherently. In this third case his intention was to eliminate both extremes of nihilism and eternalism at the same time.

STANZA 45

1)/gal te 'byung ba'i rang bzhin gzugs/
/'byung las gzugs ni 'byung ba min/
/rang las 'byung min gzhan las kyang/
/'byung min di phyin med min nam/

1)The wording of stanza 45 in the root text differs quite markedly from the wording of stanza 45 in the Candrakīrti commentary, though there is no difference in meaning. We prefer the wording in the Candrakīrti version, which is given above. The version in the root text is given below.

/gal te gzugs ni rang 'byung bzhin/
/gzugs de 'byung las 'byung ma yin/
/rang las 'byung min ma yin nam/
/gzhan las kyang min de med phyir/

Neither does inherently existent *form,* having *the nature of elements, arise from elements nor from itself* and *not even from others. Therefore, it does not exist,* does it?

When we say that form lacks inherent existence the opponent argues that this is wrong because the Buddha has said that form arises from the four elements. This statement of the Buddha expresses clearly how form lacks inherent existence because of its arising in dependence upon the elements. Also, we argue that if inherently existing form has arisen from the four elements, then we must consider whether or not form has the same nature as the four elements. If it is said that form has the same nature as the four elements then it would have arisen by itself. But here form refers to the material body (whereas in other cases form refers to shape and color), which can be seen, while the four elements can be experienced by the body sense but not seen, so these must be different. Because they are different they cannot have the same inherent nature, so then inherently existing form cannot have arisen by itself. Also, if the four elements have a different nature then the inherently existing form, in that case, after eliminating them, form should still be existent, but this is not the case, so form does not exist inherently other than the elements. As form is dependent on the four elements, then it exists conventionally but not inherently.

STANZA 46

/gcig la bzhi nyid yod min cing/
/bzhi la'ng gcig nyid yod min pas/
/gzugs ni 'byung ba chen po bzhi/
/rgyur byas nas grub ji ltar yod/

A form *cannot have* the *fourfold nature* of the elements because if the form has four elements then it will be fourfold *and* the *four* elements *cannot have* a *singular* form or else they will become one like form, *so how can form arise from the four great elements as its cause?*

Here again, form refers to the body. The question is, how can the four great elements be the cause of the body? There are two reasons why this is not possible. If form depends upon the nature of the four inherently existing elements then it should be like the four elements, that is, it should have a fourfold nature. Alternatively, the four inherently existing elements would have to have a singular nature, like form. But because form doesn't have a fourfold nature like the elements, and because the elements do not have a singular nature like form, therefore, how could form arise from the four inherently existing elements as its cause? In fact, form exists conventionally through a dependent relationship with the four elements.

STANZA 47

In the previous stanzas we have refuted the inherent existence of form, but now the opponent asserts that form must have inherent existence because it can be apprehended by a mind. Nāgārjuna answers:

> /shin tu mi 'dzin phyir de med/
> /rtags las she na 1)rtags de'ng med/
> /rgyu dang rkyen las skyes pa'i phyir/
> /2)rtags med par yang mi rigs so/
>   1)P:rtag 2)P:rtag

Form *is not apprehended* as inherently existing, *so therefore* the form *does not exist* inherently. *If it is said* that the inherent existence of form is understood 3)*by the mind* which apprehends it, then *such a mind does not exist* inherently *because* it *has arisen from causes and conditions so* it *cannot be used as a reason for proving* the inherent existence of a form.
  3)Lit: rtags las; from a mark.

If, says Nāgārjuna, a form were to be perceived or

apprehended, then, as you assert, that form should have inherent existence. But it is not apprehended at all, so form lacks inherent existence. What reason could you put forth to prove that the inherent existence of form can be apprehended by mind? The opponent answers that we know something is a form because we first perceive it as a form and then we can get an image of a form in our mind and we can think "that is a form." So, says the opponent, unless we can perceive a form we cannot think "it is a form" and with this reason we can understand how form is perceived, and since it is perceived, it has inherent existence.

But, says Nāgārjuna, what lacks inherent existence cannot be used as a proof of something else having inherent existence. Since the mind which is doing the apprehending lacks inherent existence because it is dependent on causes and conditions so too must the form which is apprehended by that mind lack inherent existence. Moreover, the reasons put forth by that non-inherently existing mind must also lack inherent existence, so they too are not suitable for proving an argument about the inherent existence of something. Therefore, because the mind does not apprehend the form as inherently existing, so it does not exist inherently.

STANZA 48

Again, refuting the assertion of the opponent that if a mind apprehends a form then the form must exist, Nāgārjuna says:

/gal te blo des gzugs 'dzin na/
/rang 1)gi rang bzhin la 'dzin 'gyur/
/rkyen las skyes pas yod min pas/
/yang dag gzugs med ji ltar 'dzin/
1)P:gis

If a mind apprehends a form with inherent existence then the mind will apprehend its own nature. Such a mind *has arisen from* causes and *conditions, so* it is a dependent arising which *lacks* inherent *existence.* In

the same way, *form does not exist truly, so how can*
that mind *apprehend* a form with true existence?

If a mind which apprehends form were to exist inherently
such a mind and its object — form — will have the same
inherent nature and the mind would apprehend its own
nature. If mind apprehends its own nature it would follow
that the subjective mind and its object become inseparably
one and we cannot find the distinction between the two: one
as perceiver and the other as that which is perceived. But if
such a mind does not apprehend itself then how can it
apprehend another? It will be like a stone or vase which
does not apprehend an other as it cannot apprehend itself.
Because mind is a dependent arising, how can it apprehend
an inherently existing form; in fact, it cannot.

STANZA 49

Although we have explained how the mind which
apprehends and the form apprehended do not exist inherently, still the opponent maintains that a person can
apprehend a form with true existence because in the Sūtra
Piṭaka it is explained how in the three times forms can be
apprehended. Thus, says the opponent, form must exist.
We agree that form may be apprehended, but not inherently existing form, while the opponent asserts that inherently
existing form can be apprehended. Nāgārjuna then argues
as follows:

/ji skad bshad gzugs skyes 1)pa'i blo'i/
/skad cig skad cig gis mi 'dzin/
/'das dang ma 'ongs 2)pa gzugs kyang/
/de 3)yis ji ltar rtogs 4)bar 'gyur/
    1)P:pa 2)D:gzugs kyi ni 3)P:yi 4)D:ngar

The kind of form, which has *arisen* but not ceased to
exist, that I have *explained is not apprehended by each
moment of the mind* in the present. Therefore, *how
can such a mind apprehend forms* of the *past* and also
the *future?*

Both mind and form are momentary phenomena. Every moment of the mind (e.g., eye consciousness) in the present is unable to apprehend a form which has arisen but not ceased because of its extremely short duration. If the opponent asserts that the passage of moments between the occurrence of the form and its apprehension by the eye consciousness is not a problem because the eye consciousness can apprehend a form in the past or the future, we say that this is impossible because the form of the past has disintegrated and the form of the future is yet to arise. Thus both are non-existent at the time of the eye consciousness of the present, so how can they be apprehended?

STANZA 50

In the preceeding stanzas we explained how form doesn't exist inherently. Now the opponent argues that since the form entrance (i.e., form as an object of perception) exists, so form should exist. Moreover, he says, form exists inherently because color and shape exist inherently. Nāgārjuna refutes this assertion beginning from the position that the form entrance is coordinated to color and shape and cannot be identified individually if the color and shape of forms are excluded. If color and shape lack inherent existence, so must form and then so must the form entrance.

/gang tshe nam yang kha dog dang/
/dbyibs dag tha dad nyid med pas/
/de dag tha dad 'dzin yod min/
/gzugs de gcig tu'ng grags pa min/

In all times color and shape do not exist as two *different* things. If they were to exist as two different things then a mind could apprehend shape without considering color or color without considering shape. Because *these* two do not exist as two different things, so therefore there *is not* a mind which *apprehends* 1)shape without taking color into consideration nor color without taking shape into consideration. 2)*In the world*, a *form* is known to be *singular;* if its shape and color were to exist as two different things then the form would appear to the world as two instead of one.

1)Lit: tha dad; distinction, difference, separatedness. 2)Lit: grags pa min; isn't known.

Form refers to shape and color. If it exists inherently, does it exist as one with shape and color or different from them? If they exist as one, in that case both shape and color would mean the same thing, which means shape and color become undifferentiable. But if they exist differently, in that case also, form should exist individually after excluding its shape and color. An eye consciousness should be able to perceive a form without considering its shape just as we see a vase without depending on a pillar or woolen cloth for seeing it. But that is not the case. Therefore, form cannot exist inherently, so also its shape and color. Doesn't the world know that a form is singular? If it exists inherently, either its shape and color must be one, as it is, or it should be two, as are its shape and color. In reality, they are mutually dependent on each other and thus lack inherent existence.

STANZA 51

The opponent now asserts that form exists inherently because an eye can perceive it. Nāgārjuna refutes this by asking, does the subject have eye consciousness or does the object have eye consciousness?

/mig blo mig la yod min te/
/gzugs la yod min bar na med/
/gzugs dang mig la brten nas de/
/yongs su rtog pa log pa yin/

The *eye has no consciousness* because the eye is a form but eye consciousness is formless and that which is formless cannot adhere to form. In the same way the *form* which is observed *has no* eye consciousness, *nor is* it *between* eye and form. *Because* eye consciousness is generated *in dependence on eye and form,* if it is apprehended as having inherent existence, that is a *mistaken conception.*

If form is inherently existent, does the eye sense or the form have eye consciousness? Also, does eye consciousness exist in between the eye sense and form? If form as an object has eye consciousness it means eye consciousness cannot be formless because of its being inseparably one with the inherently existing form. This is incorrect. But now if it is different from form that means there is no relationship at all between the two. Obviously it cannot exist between the eye sense and the form. Because of their mutual dependence, eye sense, form and eye consciousness are empty of inherent existence and apprehending them to exist inherently is a mistaken conception.

STANZA 52

/gal te mig bdag 1)mi mthong na/
/2)des gzugs mthong bar ji ltar 'gyur/
/de phyir mig dang gzugs bdag med/
/skye mched lhag ma'ng de bzhin no/
   1)P,D:mig 2)D:de

When the *eye does not see itself, how can it see forms? Therefore* the *eye and* the *forms do not have self-*existence and the *remaining entrances* should be understood *in the same way.*

If an eye could perceive a form with inherent existence then, as we have previously shown, it would be able to perceive itself. This does not mean that the eye sense organ should be able to perceive itself as an object which is an eye sense organ. Rather, this means that if the eye could perceive a form with inherent existence then it too would have inherent existence and could therefore perceive its own inherent existence. By this we mean that if the eye existed inherently it would not need to depend on any other factor or thing in order to perceive its object. Since it wouldn't need to depend on any other factor or thing it would be able to perceive itself. However, it can't perceive itself, so it is non-inherently existent, and by this logic it also can't perceive the inherent existence of any other object. Because perception, eye and object are mutually interdependent it means they lack inherent existence, and whatever depends on something non-inherently existent must also be non-inherently existent. For our opponent, lack of inherent existence means non-existence. So from the perspective of his assertions, the eye would not be able to perceive form at all.

However the eye does, as we know, perceive form. If it is not perceiving inherently existing form then it must be perceiving non-inherently existing form, and since the one depends on the other, so both eye and form lack inherent existence or self-existence.

The same logic can be applied to the remaining five entrances and prove their non-inherent existence.

STANZA 53

> /mig ni rang bdag nyid kyis stong/
> /de ni gzhan 1)bdag gis kyang stong/
> /gzugs kyang de bzhin stong pa ste/
> /skye 2)mched lhag ma'ng de bzhin no/
>   1)P:dag 2)P:de ched

> The *eye is devoid of* its *own self-existent nature. It is also devoid of* the *self*-existent nature of an *other. In the same way, form is devoid of its* own self-existent nature as well as that of *another. And it is the same* with the *rest* of the *entrances.*

When it is said that eye and form are devoid of the self-existent nature of another, this refers to the fact that consciousness, eye and form arise together and the "other" referred to are consciousness and eye in the case of form, and consciousness and form in the case of the eye.

STANZA 54

In the previous stanza we showed how eye consciousness and form do not have inherent existence. The opponent, however, still asserts that they exist inherently because eye consciousness does arise in dependence on the contact of eye and form.

> /gang tshe gcig reg lhan cig 'gyur/
> /de tshe gzhan rnams stong pa nyid/
> /stong pa'm mi stong mi 1)bsten la/
> /mi stong pa yang 2)stong mi brten/
>   1)D:stong 2)P:brten, D:rten

> *When any* of the six internal entrances *arises simultaneously* with *contact, at that time* the *rest* of the entrances *will be devoid* of the nature of contact. The rest of the entrances which are *devoid* of the nature of contact *do not depend* on the nature of contact. *That which is not devoid* of the nature of contact *will not depend on* that which is *devoid* of the nature of contact.

Only one of the entrances at a time can arise simultaneously with contact; at that moment the rest of the entrances are not in contact with their objects. Now, if it is asserted that contact has inherent existence, then that which depends on it, the eye entrance, must also have inherent existence. In this case the eye entrance and contact have the same nature, which is their inherent existence, and these two would be inseparable.

The other five entrances have not, at this moment, arisen and each of them is different than the eye entrance. For example, the eye entrance and the ear entrance are different. Now if the eye entrance arises with contact and has inherent existence, then the other five entrances which are different than the eye entrance and have not arisen at that moment (and so are devoid of the nature of contact) must lack inherent existence, for what does not have the nature of contact does not depend on what has the nature of contact. But what has inherent existence must exist inherently at all times, so these five entrances can never exist inherently. But since this example could have been used for the ear entrance, then in that case the eye entrance would lack inherent existence! So this shows that the argument is fallacious and neither the entrances nor contact exists inherently.

STANZA 55

/ngo bo mi nas yod min pas/
/gsum 'dus pa yod ma yin no/
/de 1)bdag nyid 2)kyi reg med 3)pas/
/de 4)tshe tshor ba yod ma yin/
   1)P:dag 2)D:gyis 3)D:nga 4)P:che, D:cha

The eye, eye consciousness and its object arise and immediately disintegrate, so they *cannot exist* as abiding *in* their *natures and so those three cannot assemble.* 5)When these three cannot assemble, *contact cannot exist and* if contact cannot exist, *so there cannot be feeling.*
   5)Lit: de bdag nyid kyi, by those (having no) self-nature.

If an eye consciousness were to exist inherently, in that case, it might be possible for the three — eye, eye consciousness and its object — to have an assembled nature from which contact could arise. But eye, eye consciousness and object are all momentary phenomena without self-nature. Since they disintegrate immediately after they arise there is not time for the three of them to assemble and for contact to occur between them. Also, since they do not have their own natures as existing by themselves, how could they come together and have an assembled inherent nature?

If these three cannot assemble in this way, then how can there be any contact with a nature of inherent existence? Since feeling depends on contact, so feeling must also lack inherent existence.

STANZA 56

/nang dang phyi yi skye mched la/
/brten nas rnam par shes pa 1)'byung/
/de 2)lta bas na rnam shes ni/
/smig rgyu sgyu ma bzhin du stong/
   1)P:'gyung, D:'gyur 2)P:ltang, D:ltar

Consciousness arises in dependence on internal and external entrances. Because *consciousness* arises in dependence on the entrances, *so it is like a mirage* and an *illusion* which *are devoid* of inherent existence.

Still, the opponent asserts that the entrances do exist inherently because consciousness arises in dependence on those entrances. We argue, however, that if consciousness were to exist inherently then it could not arise in dependence on internal and external entrances, because what is inherently existent must be independent. As consciousness only arises in dependence upon external entrances such as form and internal entrances such as an eye, it is clear that it is empty of inherent existence. It is like a mirage which appears as water or a magician's illusion which appears as horses and elephants.

Because consciousness lacks inherent existence it is like a mirage, which is something which exists, but not in the way it appears to exist. It is this very mode of the appearance of an object to our eye consciousness which is the thing which Nāgārjuna wishes to refute.

STANZA 57

/rnam shes shes bya la brten 1)na/
/'byung la shes bya yod ma yin/

/shes bya shes pa med pa'i phyir/
/de phyir shes pa po nyid med/
   1)D:nas

Consciousness cannot arise without taking its object, so it *depends on* the *object of knowledge.* The *object of knowledge cannot arise* without depending on the consciousness which apprehends it, and therefore because they exist in a mutually dependent·way both of them *lack* inherent *existence.* The *object of knowledge* and the *apprehension* of the object *do not exist* inherently, *therefore* the *person who knows* the object *does not exist* inherently.

Now, the opponent still believes that even though the object of knowledge and the apprehension of the object don't exist inherently, since there are persons who know the object, therefore these persons do have inherent existence. We argue that if the object of knowledge and the apprehension of the object of knowledge don't exist inherently, how can the person who knows the object exist inherently?

STANZA 58

/thams cad mi rtag yang na ni/
/mi rtag pa yang rtag pa med/
/dngos 1)po rtag dang mi rtag nyid/
/'gyur na de lta ga la yod/
   1)D:bo

Buddha has seen no essence in composite phenomena with inherent existence so he said that *all* composite phenomena *are impermanent,* so therefore they are devoid of inherent existence, *or* because he said that all composite phenomena are *impermanent, so* how could they 2)*exist* inherently in the nature of *permanent* phenomena? If *phenomena* were to have inherent existence they should either be *permanent*

or impermanent: how can there be phenomena which
are both permanent and impermanent at the same
time?
    2)Lit: rtag pa med; do not exist permanently.

Because Buddha has seen reality he has said that all
composite things are impermanent. The opponent mistakenly believes that this means that impermanence has
inherent existence. We refute this.

Because all composite things are impermanent, they lack
inherent existence. When Buddha says that all composite
things are impermanent he also implies that permanent
phenomena lack inherent existence.

STANZA 59

/sdug dang mi sdug phyi ci log/
/rkyen las chags sdang gti mug dngos/
/'byung phyir chags sdang gti mug dang/
/rang bzhin gyis ni yod ma yin/

Through superimposition one develops the three
distorted preconceptions toward *pleasing, repulsive*
and neutral objects, which respectively *cause attachment, hatred* and *closed-mindedness. Because* they
arise in dependence on these conditions, the
1)*essential nature of attachment, hatred* and *closed-
mindedness is without* inherent *existence.*
    1)rang bzhin.

Superimposition (sgro 'dogs) is an imposition or imputation of an extreme conception upon a basis of imputation,
which is a supposed object. It is actually a process of over-
estimating the nature of such a basis in either of two extreme directions. An example would be the seeing of
permanence in what is actually a transitory phenomenon.
Out of this superimposing process we develop attachment
for what appears to be pleasing, hatred for what appears
repulsive, and closed-mindedness or confusion for what

appears to be neutral. Such preconceptions (pleasing, repulsive, and neutral thoughts and feelings) are mere imputations without inherent existence, because they arise in dependence on the condition of superimposition.

STANZA 60

/gang phyir de nyid la chags shing/
/de la she sdang de la rmongs/
/de phyir rnam par rtog pas bskyed/
/rtog de'ng yang dag nyid du med/

A pleasing object does not exist inherently because some persons develop *attachment towards it,* others develop *hatred towards it,* and still others develop *closed-mindedness towards it. Therefore* such qualities of the object are merely *created by preconceptions, and these preconceptions* also 1)*do not exist inherently* because they develop from superimposition.

1)Lit: yang dag nyid du med; do not truly exist.

Here Nāgārjuna carries the argument in the previous stanza a step further. At a given moment three different observers may demonstrate the three distorted preconceptions towards the same object. This shows that the qualities associated with an object do not inhere in it, but are imputed to it through the power of the preconceptions. For instance, an attractive thing does not exist inherently because its quality — attractiveness — is fabricated by a concept. Whatever is imputed upon it lacks inherent existence as it is created by a thought (a preconception). Such a preconception has to be empty of inherent existence because of its dependent arising. From that it also follows that the three poisonous delusions (attachment, hatred and ignorance) which are produced by such distorted preconceptions lack inherent existence and so do the actions motivated by them. Also, if a pleasant thing exists inherently it should be seen as pleasant by all people, which does not stand true as some see it as repulsive and generate hatred towards it, whereas some others see it neither as pleasant nor as unpleasant and maintain a neutral feeling. If this object lacks inherent existence, so must the thought-consciousness which imputes qualities to it, for they both arise in dependence, as Nāgārjuna states in the next stanza.

STANZA 61

/brtag bya gang de yod ma yin/
/brtag bya med rtog ga la yod/
/de phyir brtag bya rtog pa dag
/rkyen las skyes phyir stong pa nyid/

Whatever may be an *object of examination does not exist* inherently. As that *object of examination does not exist* inherently, *how can* the *thought-consciousness* of that non-inherently existing object *exist* inherently? *Therefore, because* the *object of examination* and the *thought-consciousness arise from* causes and *conditions*, they *are empty* of inherent existence.

STANZA 62

Having demonstrated in the previous stanza that thought-consciousness itself is without inherent existence, Nāgārjuna now turns to the heart of his discourse, which is its implications for liberation.

/de nyid rtogs 1)pas phyin ci log
/bzhi las byung ba'i ma rig med/
/de med na ni 'du byed rnams/
/mi 'byung lhag ma'ng de bzhin no/
　1)P:ba'i

The *mind* which directly understands emptiness is an unmistaken mind which *eliminates* the *ignorance* that *arises from* the *four* evil *preconceptions*. *Without that* ignorance the *karmic formations will not arise*, and *so neither* will the *remaining* limbs.

When the mind directly sees the lack of inherent existence both of things and of itself (that is, their emptiness), then it is unmistaken. Such an unmistaken mind eliminates ignorance arising from the preconceptions by seeing the ultimate nature of things, thereby preventing the arising of new karmic formations, and so freeing one from the cyclic existence whose arising is described by the twelve limbs of dependent origination.

Reasoning, such as that employed in the *Seventy Stanzas on Emptiness,* is a necessary step in developing an unmistaken mind. This is because although one can directly perceive the gross nature of an object, one must first reason about the subtle nature of the object, which is its lack of inherent existence, before one can develop the direct perceiver which directly perceives this subtle nature of an object. A thought-consciousness which correctly analyzes the subtle nature of an object is converted through meditation into an unmistaken direct perceiver which knows the subtle nature of an object, which is a mere vacuity.

The conversion of thought-consciousness into an unmistaken direct perceiver can only be accomplished through meditation. This meditation must follow the earlier reasoning about the subtle nature of an object, for this has shown the practitioner what is to be meditated upon. A two-step process is being described here which a metaphor will help to clarify. Suppose a magician were to come to a crossroads and, setting up some sticks which were found there, magically convert them into horses and elephants. Attracting an audience, he bids the animals to do tricks for the entertainment of the onlookers. When the crowd disperses, the magician goes on his way, leaving the sticks behind. If some person were now to pass by the crossroads he would know nothing of the earlier performance, and would simply see some sticks at the crossroads.

In this metaphor, the magician sees a mere appearance of horses and elephants but does not cling to them as horses and elephants for he knows that he created them. Similarly, the practitioner who has understood emptiness through modes of profound reasoning does not cling to phenomena as having true existence although they appear to exist truly. Ordinary people hold things to exist truely and phenomena appear to them in such a manner. This is similar to the type of appearance and the perception of people who watch the magic illusion. Now as to the one who has eliminated ignorance and sees emptiness directly, things neither appear to him as truly existent nor does he cling to them as having true existence. His position is similar to that of the person who has not watched the magic illusion, he won't see either the appearance of illusory horses and elephants or have any clinging to them as horses and elephants.

The magician is also analogous to the practitioner who has entered the Path of Accumulation (tshogs lam). He gains his understanding through hearing and contemplation, using a mental image of emptiness. Then, entering the Path of Preparation, he utilizes meditation in order to progress through four levels, successively removing the mental image at each level. When it is completely gone and the practitioner perceives emptiness directly, he has entered the Path of Seeing (mthong lam) and is called an "Ārya." What he sees and the state he has attained is indicated in the next stanza.

STANZA 63

/gang gang la brten skye ba'i dngos/
/de de med pas de mi skye/
/dngos dang dngos med 'dus byas dang/
/'dus ma byas 'di mya ngan 'das/

Anything which *arises in dependence on any* causes will *not arise without those* causes. Hence, *functional things* in the form of *produced* phenomena and *non-functional things* as *unproduced* phenomena would be empty of inherent existence which is the natural state of *nirvāṇa*.

Ignorance as a cause produces karmic formations and so forth, which are functional things, but these cannot arise without that ignorance. When such functional things do not exist, their opposite nature, non-functional things, cannot exist. Therefore functional things in the form of composite phenomena and non-functional things as non-composite phenomena are devoid of an inherently existent nature; this is known as natural nirvāṇa. If a person develops the wisdom which understands this and acquaints himself more and more with this wisdom, assisted by the method of repeated meditation, he or she can attain the state of non-abiding nirvāṇa which is free from the extremes of cyclic existence and solitary peace.

The two extremes of eternalism and nihilism do not exist but there are people who fall on these extremes. However, the two extremes of cyclic existence and solitary peace which are posited from the conventional point of view are existent and also there are people who fall on these extremes. The nonabiding nirvāṇa of the Mahāyāna Vehi. .e is free from these extremes.

STANZA 64

/rgyu rkyen las skyes dngos po rnams/
/yang dag nyid du rtog pa gang/
/de ni ston pas ma rig gsungs/
/de las yan 1)lag bcu gnyis 'byung/
　1)P:yag

The Teacher, Buddha, *said* that *the conception of true existence* of *functional things* which *arise from causes* and *conditions is ignorance. From this ignorance arise* the *twelve* dependent *limbs.*

Things which are produced by causes and conditions do not exist truly or inherently. The conception of the self of phenomena refers to the ignorance of grasping at the true existence of aggregates contaminated by actions and delusion. The twelve dependent limbs arise from this ignorance.

STANZA 65

/dngos po stong par de rtogs 1)na/
/yang dag mthong phyir rmongs mi 'gyur/
/de ni ma rig 'gog pa yin/
/de las yan lag bcu gnyis 'gag/
   1)D:nas

Understanding the non-inherent existence of *things*
means *seeing* the *reality* [i.e., *emptiness*] which *elim-*
inates ignorance about the reality of things. *This*
brings about the *cessation* of *ignorantly* grasping at
an apparently true existence. *From that* the *twelve*
limbs of dependent origination *cease*.

In this and the previous stanza we have Nāgārjuna's
restatement of the four noble truths. The twelve limbs are
suffering existence. Their source is ignorant grasping. Suffering ceases when ignorant grasping ceases. Seeing reality
is the path. The reality of things is then described in the
next stanza in terms familiar to us from the *Mūlamadhyama-*
kakārikā and the Perfection of Wisdom sūtras.

STANZA 66

/'du byed dri za'i grong 1)khyer dang/
/sgyu ma 2)smig rgyu skra shad dang/
/dbu 3)ba chu bur sprul 4)pa dang/
/rmi lam mgal me'i 'khor lo mtshungs/
   1)D:khyeng 2)P:mig 3)D:pa 4)P:ma

Produced phenomena are similar to a village of gan-
dharvas, an illusion, a hair net in the eyes, foam, a
bubble, an emanation, a dream, and a circle of light
produced by a whirling firebrand.

A less metaphoric description of the reality of things is
found in the next two stanzas.

STANZA 67

/rang bzhin gyis ni 'ga' yang med/
/'di la dngos po med pa'ng med/
/rgyu dang rkyen las skyes ba yi/
/dngos dang dngos med stong ba yin/

There is *nothing* which *exists inherently*. *In that fashion even non-functional things do not exist*. Therefore, *functional things which arise from causes and conditions* as well as *non-functional things are empty* of inherent existence.

STANZA 68

/dngos kun rang bzhin stong 1)pas na/
/de bzhin gshegs pa mtshungs med pas/
/rten cing 'brel par 'byung ba 'di/
/dngos po rnams su nye bar bstan/
  1)D: bas

Because all things are empty of *inherent existence* the *Peerless Tathāgata has shown* the emptiness of inherent existence of *dependent arising* as the reality *of all things*.

Stanza 67 lays the logical groundwork for stanza 68, but it does seem rather superfluous, as stanza 63 has already made the same argument. Indeed, although this stanza appears in the root verses and in the "autocommentary," it is missing from both the Candrakīrti and Parahita commentaries, suggesting that it may be an interpolation. At any rate, stanza 68 is very interesting because it is such a clear statement of the actual nature of the reality whose conventional aspect was metaphorically described in stanza 66. As we see, it is quite free from extremes. By asserting dependent arising, nihilism is avoided, and by asserting the emptiness of inherent existence, eternalism is avoided. The reality revealed by the Buddha in the middle view is the empty nature of dependent arising. Its reverse face is the conventional appearance of things. In a certain sense the two complement each other, like concave and convex, because they are two aspects of one reality. In the next stanza this complementarity is implied by the postulating of a single limit for all reality. This naturally leads to a further discussion of the Buddha's use of conventional expressions when teaching about this reality.

STANZA 69

/dam pa'i don ni der zad de/
/'jig rten ngor byas tha snyad dag/
/sna tshogs thams cad rdzogs sangs rgyas/
/bcom ldan 'das kyis 1)bden brtags mdzad/
   1)D:brten brtag

Ultimate reality is contained within the *limit* of the non-inherent existence of a thing. For that reason, the *Accomplished Buddha, the Subduer, has imputed various terms in the manner of the world* through comparison.

Reality is not beyond the limit of what is known by a valid direct perceiver. This limit must also subsume conventional reality. Within this limit the Buddha makes two kinds of comparisons. One is to examine the various things of conventional reality, to determine whether the names used to designate these objects are actually suitable for this purpose. In the second case, he compares the different aspects of an object to each other and to their names. These comparisons require that the Buddha utilize the different conventional terms used by the people of the world in order to examine the objects which they believe to exist. This process will eventually lead to the creation of a mental image of emptiness whose actual limit corresponds to that of reality. But in this process some people may become confused and, not understanding that the Buddha only uses these conventionalities for the sake of comparison, may take them to be realities, though actually they are merely imputed for the sake of analysis. This problem is described in the next stanza.

STANZA 70

/'jig rten pa yi chos bstan mi 'jig cing/
/yang dag nyid du nam yang chos 1)bstan med/
/de bzhin gshegs 2)pas gsungs pa ma rig pas/
/de las dri med brjod pa 'di las skrag/
    1)D:bsten 2)P:psa

What is *shown* conventionally *to the world* appears to be *without disintegration, but* the Buddha has *never* actually *shown* anything *with true existence. Those who do not understand what is explained by the Tathā-gata* to be conventionally existent and empty of the sign of true existence *are frightened by this teaching.*

Here we see that when making comparisons the Buddha and Nāgārjuna seem to speak as if things were permanent, that is, do not disintegrate, but this is only because conventional expressions make things seem permanent. Such permanence would imply true existence for things, which they never assert. People who make such interpretations merely demonstrate their lack of understanding of the Buddha's intentions. Furthermore, many of these people have a dangerous misunderstanding of the middle way, believing that non-existence is being taught, when actually non-inherent existence is being taught. They have fallen into the extreme of the nihilistic view, misinterpreting emptiness as indicating actual non-existence, and this nihilistic attitude causes them to be fearful when they hear the Buddha teach about non-inherent existence. Another misinterpretation would be to take the Buddha's teaching about causality at face value, forgetting his chief underlying thought. This is discussed in the next stanza.

STANZA 71

/'di la brten nas 'di 'byung zhes/

/'jig rten tshul 'di mi 'gog cing/
/1)gang brten rang bzhin med 2)pas de/
/ji ltar yod 'gyur de nyid nges/
　　1)P:kang 2)P:bas

It is known in the *way* of the *world that "this arises in
dependence on that." Such* statements *are not refuted.*
But *whatsoever* arises *dependently does not exist inherently,* and *how can that* non-inherent existence
itself *have* inherent *existence? In fact,* that non-
inherent existence *must definitely* not exist inherently!

Here Nāgārjuna reminds his auditors that causality,
which in reality is dependent arising, is itself without inherent existence. It would also be a mistake to believe that the
non-inherent existence of dependent arising itself had true
existence, when in actuality it too must be without inherent
existence. In another context this is known as the emptiness
of emptiness. Both are refutations of a subtle eternalist
interpretation of a teaching meant to refute eternalism.

In the last two stanzas of the *Seventy Stanzas on Emptiness,* Nāgārjuna moves on from this point and summarizes
the way in which his middle view leads to a nirvāṇa which is
superior to the nirvāṇa of the lesser vehicle because it does
not postulate the extreme view which asserts an actual
non-cyclic existence.

STANZA 72

/dad ldan de nyid 1)chos 2)la brtson/
/3)tshul 'di rigs pas rjes 4)dpogs gang/
/5)rten med chos 6)'ga' 7)bstan pa yi/
/srid dang srid min spangs nas zhi/
　　1)P:tshol 2)D:lar rtson 3)P:chu la 4)P:dbogs
　　5)D:brten 6)P,D:'gal 7)D:brtan

Those who have faith in the teaching of emptiness *will
strive* for it through a number of different *kinds* of
reasoning. *Whatever they have understood* about it in

terms of non-inherent existence, they *clarify* this for others, which helps others to attain 8)*nirvāṇa by abandoning* grasping at the apparently true existence of *cyclic existence and non-cyclic existence.*

8)Lit: zhi; tranquility.

STANZA 73

/'di dag rkyen 'di las 1)rig nas/
/lta ngan dra ba kun ldog des/
/chags rmongs khong khro spangs pa'i phyir/
/ma gos mya ngan 'das pa thob/
   1)D:rigs

By seeing these internal and external phenomena arising *from* causes and *conditions* they will *eliminate* the *whole network of wrong views.* With the elimination of wrong views they will have *abandoned attachment, closed-mindedness* and *hatred* and thereby *attain nirvāṇa unstained* by wrong views.

The clarification for others which is referred to in stanza 72 is not considered by Tibetans to be an act of compassion, or of bodhicitta, but a simple offering of the teaching which is an offshoot of the practitioner's own striving for understanding through reasoning. Tibetans hold two views on Nāgārjuna's teaching about great compassion. One group asserts that compassion is implied in texts such as the *Mūlamadhyamakakārikā* and the *Seventy Stanzas on Emptiness*, while another group asserts that such texts are strictly philosophical and that Nāgārjuna's teachings about compassion are to be found in other texts, such as *Ratnāvalī*, or *Sūtrasamuccaya*. In any case, whatever our opinion on this subject may be, it is clear that here, in the concluding fifteen stanzas of the *Seventy Stanzas on Emptiness*, Nāgārjuna has demonstrated the practical implications of adopting the correct view of the middle way. For this view, implemented by meditative practice, will free the yogi from grasping after cyclic existence and set him on the path to nirvāṇa.

THE COLOPHON

/stong nyid bdun cu 1)pa'i tshig le'ur byas pa zhes
bya ba/slob dpon 'phags pa klu sgrub kyis mdzad pa
rdzogs so/lo tsa' ba gzhon nu mchog dang/ 2)gnyan
dharma grags dang khu'i 'gyur dag las don dang
tshig bzang du bris pa'o
1)P omits 2)D:snyan dar ma

These *Seventy Stanzas* Explaining How Phenomena
Are *Empty* Of Inherent Existence have been *written
by* the *Teacher Ārya Nāgārjuna* and *compiled* by an
unknown editor who referred to the *better wordings
and meanings of* the *translations by* the *translators
Gzhon nu mchog, Gnyan dharma grags and Khu.*

Nāgārjuna's seventy three stanzas were translated into
English in the years 1982 and 1983 by the Venerable Geshe
Sonam Rinchen, the Venerable Tenzin Dorjee and David
Ross Komito at the Library of Tibetan Works and Archives
in Dharamsala, India. The commentary on the seventy
three stanzas is based on the oral explanations given by
Geshe Sonam Rinchen while the translation was in progress and later edited by David Komito. The root stanzas
and commentary were then orally retranslated into Tibetan
and corrected by Geshe Sonam Rinchen. Our translation
and interpretation of the *Seventy Stanzas on Emptiness* primarily follows the traditions of Sera Monastery, Lhasa,
Tibet, and that given by Candrakīrti in his *Shūnyatāsaptativṛtti* (*sTong pa nyid bdun cu pa'i 'grel pa*) and secondarily
follows that given by Parahita in his *Shūnyatāsaptativivṛtti*
(*sTong pa nyid bdun cu pa'i rnam par bshad pa*). Italicized
words in the English translation of the root stanzas correspond to those Tibetan words which actually appear in the
Tibetan root stanzas; words which are not italicized in the
English translation of the root stanzas are interpolations
placed in the stanzas in order to clarify their meaning and
are based on the commentaries and on oral tradition.

Chapter Three
The *Seventy Stanzas on Emptiness* and its Transmission

Section 3-1 Treatises by Nāgārjuna

Nāgārjuna, who seems to have lived in the second century, may be regarded as the father of philosophical Mahāyāna. We know little or nothing about the circumstances of his life, and the legendary reports to be found in the works of Tārānatha and other Tibetan historians obviously refer chiefly to a later Nāgārjuna, a Tantric and sorcerer, whose figure has become merged into that of the earlier philosophical Nāgārjuna in the consciousness of latter times.[1]

Lamentably, this situation of minimal clarity concerning the details of the life of Nāgārjuna has not altered since 1956 when these words were written. Perhaps we shall never have much in the way of facts about Nāgārjuna's life due to the general disinterest of Indians in historical or "biographical" records. K. Inada's work *Nāgārjuna* (1970) contains a bibliography which lists all the significant articles and books which deal with such biographical concerns up to the date of its publication. If we survey these citations, we find a veritable quagmire of conflicting opinions. Robinson has quoted a number of these alternative views on pages 21 to 26 of his work *Early Mādhyamika in India and China*. From his summary it can be seen that scholars are unlikely to ever establish anything like a factual biography of Nāgārjuna. I will simply follow the opinion of the majority of scholars and place his activities between 150 and 250 A.D. in India. As to the details of his life, I shall simply refer the reader to the above-mentioned references, as such details are secondary to our concerns in this book.

The difficulty of identifying the authentic works of the second century Nāgārjuna is clearly a more relevant issue, and is connected with the problem of establishing the best redaction of the text of the *Seventy Stanzas* for translation purposes. Some of the works in the Tibetan canon which are attributed to Nāgārjuna have a clearly tantric character, and obviously belong to a later Nāgārjuna. For other works, such a method of discrimination is not applicable, for their content is not so clearly tantric. The method typically adopted by the most discriminating Tibetan authorities, as well as by many modern scholars, is to only accept as authentic those works whose style and content closely agree with the *Mūlamadhyamakakārikā (Mula)*. Thus, in essence, Nāgārjuna is defined as being the author of the *Mula*, and any work which appears to accept or propose views other than those in the *Mula* is by definition authored by someone other than the Nāgārjuna of the second century, and is not considered "authentic."

Such a method has its own strengths and weaknesses. Its strength lies in its exclusion of such clearly inappropriate works as those of the tantra class, for the tantric literature is, by common agreement of all modern scholars, a development which postdates the second century Nāgārjuna, no matter in what era its roots may lie. The weakness of this method lies in the tendency of some scholars to exclude works which seem to have minimal emphasis on the prasaṅga style of exposition. Thus, if a work seems to make some positive assertions or to have some Cittamātra tendencies, for example, these scholars would have to consider it to be inauthentic. The problem here is that Nāgārjuna preceded such sectarian splits in the Mahāyāna stream which he so influenced.

As the general approach I follow in this book is to express the views of Tibetan scholars, I will also do so in regards to the question of determining what are the authentic works of Nāgārjuna. Modern scholarly opinion may disagree with the views of Tibetan scholars, and, indeed, often such modern scholarly opinion is not unanimous on a variety of issues. Lindtner has a very useful summary of the opinions of modern scholars concerning the authenticity of various works attributed to Nāgārjuna.[2] But since our general purpose is to present the Tibetan scholarly view, such disagreements only become relevant in regards to questions about the authenticity of the so-called "autocommentary" *(Shūnyatāsaptativṛtti)* to the *Seventy Stanzas* and its appropriateness for establishing the text of the *Seventy Stanzas,* so I will simply refer the interested reader to Lindtner's summary. As to the authenticity of the "autocommentary" to the *Seventy Stanzas,* I will return to this problem shortly.

If we turn to the writings of Tibetan authorities on Nāgārjuna, we will find that there is a group of works which they all attribute to him and there is a second group of works which is considered authentic by some and is rejected by others.

Bu ston, in his *History of Buddhism (Chos 'byung)* indicates that there are "... six main treatises of the Mādhyamika Doctrine (by Nāgārjuna) demonstrating that, which is expressed by the sūtras directly, or otherwise, the essential meaning (of the Doctrine)."[sic][3] They are, in the order which he gives them: *Shūnyatāsaptati, Prajñamūla, Yuktishashṭikā, Vigrahavyāvartanī, Vaidalyasūtra* and *Vyavahārasiddhi.* He further states that *Shūnyatāsaptati* expounds "... the theory of Relativity [shūnyatā] of all elements of existence, devoid of the extremities of causality (rten 'brel) and pluralism (spros pa) ..."[4]

"Tson[g] kha pa in his *Gser phren* says that the sixth work is considered by some to be the *Vyavahāra-siddhi,* by others — the *Akutobhayā* or the *Ratnāvalī*, but that it is not correct to insist upon the number of treatises as being six."[5] And he adds, in his *rTsa she ti ka chen rigs pa'i rgya mtsho*, that the *Seventy Stanzas* was written in response to an objection raised concerning chapter seven of the *Mula*.[6] Tārānatha mentions "five fundamental works" which according to Walleser does not include *Vyavahārasiddhi*.[7] According to Obermiller, this work was never translated into Tibetan.[8] Atīsha also lists the important treatises of Nāgārjuna. In his *Lamp of the Enlightenment Path (Byang chub lam gyi sgron ma)*, which is a signally important work for Tibetan Buddhism, he mentions only two works by Nāgārjuna: *Seventy Stanzas* and *Mula*.[9] In his autocommentary to that work *(Byang chub lam gyi sgron ma'i dka' 'grel)* he expands upon this grouping, stating that similar to these two are *Akutobhayā*, *Vigrahavyāvartanī*, *Yuktishashṭikā*, *Ratnāvalī*, *Mahāyānaviṃshikā*, *Akṣarashaṭaka* and *Shālistambakaṭīkā*.[10]

Taking the Chinese point of view, Robinson notes that "... the basic stanzas in the Three Treatises [i.e., the Mādhyamika school] are the work of Nāgārjuna and Āryadeva and correspond fairly closely with counterparts in Sanskrit and Tibetan ... ."[11] One of these treatises is called the *Twelve Topics (Shih-erh-men-lun*, Taisho #1568). As it quotes the eighth and nineteenth stanzas from the *Seventy Stanzas* and was itself translated by Kumārajīva, we have an established later limit for the composition of the *Seventy Stanzas* and a further attestation of its authenticity.

Thus, if we define Nāgārjuna as being the individual who authored the *Mula*, then he certainly is also the same Nāgārjuna who authored the *Seventy Stanzas*, and according to the consensus of the indigenous experts, this same person also authored *Yuktishashṭikā*, *Vigrahavyāvartanī* and *Vaidalyasūtra*. These are the agreed upon five fundamental treatises which comprise a class with certain authorship. The second class of works, accepted as authentic by some experts but not considered authentic by others would include: *Vyavahārasiddhi, Akutobhayā, Ratnāvalī, Mahāyānavimshikā, Akṣarashataka* and *Shālistambakaṭīkā.* Note that the "autocommentary" to the *Seventy Stanzas* is not included in either of these classes and that the *Akutobhayā*, which is an "autocommentary" to the *Mula*, is not considered by all authorities to have been authored by Nāgārjuna.

Besides the kārikā(s) of the *Seventy Stanzas* itself (Peking Ed. #5227), the bsTan 'gyur contains three commentaries on the *Seventy Stanzas.* The so called "autocommentary" is titled *Shūnyatāsaptativṛtti (sTong pa nyid bdun cu pa'i 'grel pa;* Peking Ed. #5231); it is attributed to Nāgārjuna. There is another and longer work of the same title which is authored by Candrakīrti (Peking Ed. #5268). The third commentary is called *Shūnyatāsaptativivṛtti (sTong pa nyid bdun cu pa'i rnam par bshad pa;* Peking Ed. #5269), and is authored by Parahita(bhadra).

All three commentaries on the *Seventy Stanzas*, as well as the isolated kārikā(s) themselves, are extant only in Tibetan.[12] Just one kārikā has survived in Sanskrit, which is quoted in the *Prasannapadā.*[13] Although the *Seventy Stanzas* was translated into Chinese, it has since been lost,[14] except for the two kārikā(s) found in the *Twelve Topic Treatise.*[15]

In addition to the redaction of the *Seventy Stanzas* kārikā(s) in an isolated form, each of the three commentaries also contains a version of the *Seventy Stanzas.* As Ruegg says, "... the variations between these versions pose a number of philological and historical problems. ... The version accompanying the Tibetan translation of Candrakīrti's commentary, and hence this commentary itself, differs from the version accompanying the commentary ascribed to Nāgārjuna; and the question arises as to whether Candrakīrti knew this commentary or recognized it to be by Nāgārjuna."[16] I will investigate some of these historical and philological problems in the balance of this chapter.

A parallel to the problem of the authenticity of the "autocommentary" to the *Seventy Stanzas* is the problem of the authenticity of the "autocommentary" to the *Mula*, called the *Aukutobhayā* (Peking Ed. #5231). This treatise was translated into German by Max Walleser in 1911.[17] As the kārikā(s) of the *Mula* are embedded in this treatise, this translation was the first appearance of the complete text of the *Mula* in a western language. Walleser accepted the attribution of Nāgārjuna's authorship, though later western scholars have taken exception to this view. De Jong does not consider this work to have been written by Nāgārjuna,[18] nor does Lindtner,[19] nor does Murti.[20] The most convincing argument is given by Obermiller:

> As concerns the Akutobhayā, we have the following interesting statement in the Stoṅ thun Bskal bzaṅ mig hbyeḍ of Khai dub ... It is said that many Tibetan authors consider the Akutobhayā to be an autocommentary (raṅ ḥgrel) of Ārya Nāgārjuna, but such an opinion shows that they have not correctly analyzed the text. Indeed, the Akutobhayā, in commenting on the 27th chapter of the Mūla-Madhyamika, quotes from the Catuḥśatikā of Āryadeva with the indication: 'It has thus been said by the venerable Āryadeva.' It is quite impossible that Nāgārjuna could have quoted the work of his pupil in such a manner ... . Similar indications are to be found likewise in Tsoṅ kha pa's Legs bśad sñin po ... where it is moreover said that Buddhapā-lita, Candrakīrti, and Bhāvaviveka have not made a single quotation from the Akutobhayā and have not even mentioned it in their works. This is likewise an argument for denying the authorship of Nāgārjuna.[21]

Thus this commentary to the *Mula* loses some of its authoritative character, though its usefulness for interpreting Mādhyamika is not necessarily thereby diminished.[22]

It may be that we face a similar situation with the "autocommentary" to the *Seventy Stanzas*. As demonstrated by the case of the "autocommentary" to the *Mula*, just because a text is attributed to Nāgārjuna does not mean that it was authored by Nāgārjuna. Following this line of reasoning, there is thus no basis for asserting that the "autocommentary" to the *Seventy Stanzas* was authored by Nāgārjuna just because the colophon makes this indication. Now this does not mean that the treatise is of no value, but it does suggest that there is no reason to believe that the "autocommentary" is Nāgārjuna's explanation of the *Seventy Stanzas* or that its version of the kārikā(s) is either older or more accurate than that in either the Candrakīrti or Parahita commentaries. As Ruegg has pointed out, it is not clear that Candrakīrti either knew of this "autocommentary" to the *Seventy Stanzas* or recognized it to be by Nāgārjuna. He may have known of it, but not accepted its authenticity, or he may not have known of it, perhaps because it was authored after Candrakīrti composed his own commentary to the *Seventy Stanzas*. Should either be the case, then the "autocommentary" loses any special significance and should simply be considered a commentary with uncertain authorship and whose date of composition is uncertain, but possibly postdates Candrakīrti (approx. 600-650 A.D.).[23] The balance of this chapter should shed some light on this problem, which is important when it comes to selecting the most appropriate redaction of the *Seventy Stanzas* for translating purposes.

Section 3-2 Translation of the Seventy Stanzas During the First Introduction of Buddhism to Tibet

Thanks to the efforts of Lalou, we can ascertain that the *Seventy Stanzas* was first translated into Tibetan during the Imperial period. In *Journal Asiatique*[1] she has translated a work from the Peking bsTan 'gyur, mDo 'grel Vol. CXXVII, which she has shown to be, in actuality, a catalogue of the Tibetan canonical collection as it existed either at the time of the Emperor Khri srong lde brtsan (775-797 A.D.), which is Lalou's position, or at the time of the Emperor Khri lde srong brtsan (799-815 A.D.), which is Tucci's position. He reviews the evidence in his *Minor Buddhist Texts*[2] and concludes that the catalogue in the bsTan 'gyur can be dated to 812 A.D. This catalogue was assembled at the "Palace of lDan kar in sTod than" by dPal brcegs and Nam mkha'i snyin po, and contains over seven hundred works.

In section XXII, titled "dbu ma'i bstan bcos la," i.e., shāstras on Mādhyamika, we find listed a translation of the *Seventy Stanzas* and one of its commentaries. They are: Lalou's #593 titled //*sTong pa nyid bdun cu pa'i chig le'ur byas pa*/ in 74 slokas; and Lalou's #594 titled //*sTong pa*

nyid bdun cu pa'i 'grel pa/ rigs pa drug cu pa'i 'grel pa/ in 280
slokas. #593 is of course our very own *Seventy Stanzas*, as is
evident from the title and from the number of stanzas.
Though our Peking edition of the *Seventy Stanzas* has 73
stanzas instead of the 74 mentioned in this catalogue, this
should not be considered as counterindicative of our conclusion. We know that portions of a text can be omitted by a
copyist and it would be no surprise if a stanza were lost
between the edition of the eighth or ninth centuries and that
of the seventeenth or eighteenth centuries, or, for that
matter, if one crept in. Indeed, stanza 67 in the Peking
edition of the *Seventy Stanzas* is omitted in the sDe dge
edition. In this case its authenticity might be confirmed by
its existence in the "autocommentary" to the *Seventy Stanzas* in both the Peking edition and the sDe dge edition (folio
120b2). On the other hand, there is no certainty that the
"autocommentary" itself was authored by Nāgārjuna. That
stanza 67 is missing in the Peking and sDe dge editions of
the Candrakīrti and Parahita commentaries suggests not
only that stanza 67 is an interpolation but also that if either
of these commentators knew of the "autocommentary" they
rejected its authority.

Furthermore, Lalou states that in regards to this catalogue of lDan kar a sloka is meant to indicate a meter of
recitation, and not a stanza or phrase per se.[3] Thus the
salutation and colophon could have been counted as two
slokas along with 72 stanzas in the body of the *Seventy
Stanzas*. Or there may have been 73 stanzas plus either the
salutation or the colophon. Unfortunately, we cannot determine what is actually included in the number 74.

Lalou's #594 presents another difficulty. As no author's
name is indicated in the catalogue, we cannot know if this
commentary is the "autocommentary," or if it is the commentary of Candrakīrti, which has the same title. As follows
from Lalou's statement about the significance of the term
"sloka" within this context, we cannot simply count up the
number of phrases in any of the currently existing commen-

taries and compare that number with the number of slokas given in the catalogue. However, as the commentary of Candrakīrti is rather extensive, we can assume with reasonable certainty that it was not indicated by this entry in the catalogue, which would have been a considerably shorter work. However, the possibility that the commentary is actually by some currently unknown author cannot be ruled out.

We can, nevertheless, adduce some other evidence which will demonstrate that, indeed, it is very likely that this commentary from the Imperial period is the same as the one which we have termed the "autocommentary." To begin with, although the colophon to the "autocommentary" in the Peking edition (#5231) mentions Nāgārjuna, it does not list any translators. However, the colophon to the sDe dge edition of this work (Tohoku #3831) states that it was translated by Jinamitra and Ye shes sde.[4] Hoffmann has identified these men as two of the compilers of *Mahāvyutpatti*.[5] This work is known to be contemporary with the reign of Khri lde srong brtsan (following Tucci, above, who dates the *Mahāvyutpatti* at 812 A.D.), and thus also the catalogue of Ldan kar. Therefore, the redaction of the autocommentary in the sDe dge edition would appear to be a copy of a work which was first translated during the Imperial period. This would seem to have survived the general destruction of texts during the Tibetan persecution of Buddhists during the ninth century. Indeed, the *Blue Annals* implies that such works had been preserved, as do modern scholars, such as Wayman.[6]

Additionally, Stein's explorations into Inner Asia and subsequent retrieval of manuscripts from Tun-huang has given us some further evidence in this matter. The India Office Library possesses a single folio in Tibetan of a work which La Vallée Poussin has identified as *Shūnyatāsaptativṛtti*.[7] The kārikā(s) commented upon are 19 through 23 inclusive. As the manuscripts in this collection are believed to be the production of translators and copyists from the

Imperial period, a comparison of these five kārikā(s) from the Tun-huang collection with the similar kārikā(s) from later editions of the bsTan 'gyur should be most informative. Therefore we include this fragment of the text below, accompanied by the corresponding kārikā(s) from Lindtner's edition of the "autocommentary."[8] As can be seen, the Tun-huang kārikā(s) are much more similar to those in the "autocommentary" then they are to those in our edition of the *Seventy Stanzas*, which are based upon the isolated kārikā(s) in the bsTan 'gyur and the embedded kārikā(s) in the Candrakīrti commentary. This further supports the view that the "autocommentary" in the bsTan 'gyur was, as indicated by its colophon, translated during the Imperial period, that it survived the destruction of texts during the ninth century, and is, most likely, the text indicated in the lDan dkar catalogue (#549).

Tun-huang:19

> /dngos dang dngos myed cig car myed/
> /dngos myed myed par dngos po myed/
> /rtag du dngos po'i dngos myed de/
> /dngos myed myed na dngos myed myed/

autocommentary:19

> /dngos dang dngos med cig car med/
> /dngos med med par dngos po med/
> /rtag tu dngos dang dngos med 'gyur/
> /dngos dang dngos po med mi 'gyur/

Tun-huang:20

> /dngos po myed par dngos myed myed/
> /bdag las ma yin gzhan las myin/
> /de lta bas na dngos po myed/
> /de myed na ni dngos myed myed/

autocommentary:20

> /dngos po med par dngos med med/

/bdag las ma yin gzhan las min/
/de lta bas na dngos po med/
/de med na ni dngos med med/

Tun-huang:21

/dngos po yod pa nyid na rtag/
/myed na nges par chad pa yin/
/[dngos po yo]d na de gnyis yin/
/de phyir dngos po khas blangs myin/

autocommentary:21

/dngos po yod pa nyid na rtag/
/med na nges par chad pa yin/
/dngos po yod na de gnyis yin/
/de'i phyir dngos po khas blangs min/

Tun-huang:22

/rgyun gyi phyir na de myed de/
/rgyu byin nas ni dngos po 'gag/
/snga ma bzhin du 'di ma grub/
/rgyu chad pa'i nyes pa 'ng yod/

autocommentary:22

/rgyun gyi phyir na de med de/
/rgyu byin nas ni dngos po 'gag/
/snga ma bzhin du 'di ma grub/
/rgyun chad pa yi nyes pa'ng yod/

Tun-huang:23

/skye 'jig gzigs pas mya ngan 'das/
/lam bstan stong nyid phyir ma yin/
/'di dag phan tsun bzlog phyir dang/
/log pa'i phyir na mthong ba yin/

autocommentary:23

/skye 'jig gzigs pas mya ngan 'das/
/lam bstan stong nyid phyir ma yin/

/'di dag phan tshun bzlog phyir dang/
/log pa'i phyir na mthong ba yin/

Returning to the catalogue of lDan kar, we find another title which follows Lalou's #593, and #594 in consecutive order. Lalou's #595 is a work which is missing from the Tibetan canon as it is currently known to us. The title of the work in the lDan kar catalogue is //*sTong pa nyid kyi sgo bcu gnyis pa/ rtsa ba dan 'grel par bcas pa*/ in 600 slokas. This may be translated as *Twelve Entrances of Shūnyatā Commented (Upon) With Root (Verses)*. Unfortunately, no author is given and beyond the title we know nothing more about this work except that it does not appear in any current editions of the bsTan 'gyur. Apparently this is the same treatise as the work in the Chinese canon called *Twelve Topic Treatise (Shih-erh-men-lun;* Taisho #1568) which we discussed earlier, an opinion shared by Lindtner and others.[9] Robinson, for example, has reconstructed the Sanskrit title of this Chinese translation as *Dvādashamukhashāstra*. Thus *Twelve Topic Treatise* is the same as *Twelve Entrances of Shūnyatā Commented Upon With Root Verses*. The Chinese version is attributed to Nāgārjuna and was, as stated earlier, translated by Kumārajīva.[10]

The text is divided into twelve chapters, each dealing with one topic: the first chapter deals with causes and conditions; the seventh chapter deals with the existent and the non-existent. Chapter one contains a stanza which turns out to be stanza 8 in the *Seventy Stanzas*, and chapter seven contains only one stanza, which turns out to be stanza 19 in the *Seventy Stanzas*.[11] Seventeen of the other stanzas in the *Twelve Topic Treatise* are identical to stanzas in the *Mula*. Robinson states that the content of this treatise "is mostly a duplication" of the *Mula*;[12] its authorship is disputed.[13]

The occurrence of *Seventy Stanzas* stanzas 8 and 19 in the *Twelve Topic Treatise* establishes an historical "later-limit" for the *Seventy Stanzas* which stands independently of any questions about the dates of Nāgārjuna's life. Robinson believes that Kumārajīva obtained a copy of the *Twelve Topic Treatise* while still in Kashgar, perhaps about 360 A.D., though he can produce no hard facts to support this assertion.[14] Inada gives the date of its translation by Kumārajīva as 409 A.D.[15] At any rate, it was certainly translated before his death in 413 A.D.

Section 3-3 Translation of the Seventy Stanzas During the Second Introduction of Buddhism to Tibet

During the "second introduction" of Buddhism to Tibet, the *Seventy Stanzas* again became a point of interest for translators rendering Mādhyamika philosophy into Tibetan. It appears that much of the initial impetus for the work on Mādhyamika came from Atīsha, whose name is intimately connected with the reintroduction. In his influential work *Lamp for the Bodhi Path* he writes:

> The reasoning of the *Shūnyatāsaptati*,
> And of works like the *Mūlamadhyamaka* also,
> Explain the proof for the emptiness
> Of inherent existence in entities.[1]

He thus recommends these works to his disciples and all later generations of Tibetan Buddhists.

If we look at the various works relating to the *Seventy Stanzas* in the bsTan 'gyur, we find that with the exception of the "autocommentary," the remaining two show the influence of Atīsha to some degree. Let us therefore now examine these texts and the translators who worked with them. They are: [1] *Seventy Stanzas* itself, *Shūnyatāsaptati-kārikānāma*; (Peking Ed. #5227); author: Nāgārjuna; translators: gZhon nu mchog, gNyan dharma grags and Khu. [2] *Shūnyatāsaptativṛtti*; (Peking Ed. #5268); author: Candrakīrti; translators; Abhayākara and Dharma grags. [3] *Shūnyatāsaptativivṛtti*; (Peking Ed. #5269); author: Parahita; translators: Parahita and gZhon nu mchog.

The first point to note is that of the three translators of the *Seventy Stanzas*, except for Khu, each of the remaining two is also a co-translator of a commentary upon the *Seventy Stanzas* root verses, and in the colophons to each of these commentaries the name of an Indian pandita is also mentioned. However, no Indian pandita's name is associated with the *Seventy Stanzas*. As each of the commentaries contain the *Seventy Stanzas* root verses they comment upon, it is my hypothesis that the root verses which are now extant under the title *Shūnyatāsaptatikārikānāma* are an edition which was compiled out of previous translations of the commentaries to the *Seventy Stanzas*. To explore this hypothesis, and also to develop some of the historical context of the translation of the *Seventy Stanzas* from Sanskrit into Tibetan during the second introduction of Buddhism to Tibet, we will turn our attention to these translators.

The colophon to *Shūnyatāsaptativivṛtti* indicates that the treatise was translated at mTho gling monastery by Parahita (who is also its author) and gZhon nu mchog. mTho gling was the center of Atīsha's initial activities in western Tibet during the years 1042 to 1045, and we know from the biography of Atīsha that Parahita accompanied him from Nālandā to mTho gling.[2] Moreover, we also know from the colophon to Peking Ed. #5633 that Atīsha and gZhon nu mchog worked together. Since we may assume that if Parahita accompanied Atīsha to mTho gling, he in all likelihood also accompanied him to central Tibet, and since we have ample evidence of gZhon nu mchog's translating activities at mTho gling with other of Atīsha's traveling companions, we may reasonably assume that *Shūnyatāsaptativivṛtti* was translated between 1042 and 1045 A.D. Since the text itself primarily explains the meaning of terms in the *Seventy Stanzas*, we may also presume that it was composed at mTho gling in the course of preparing the translation of the *Seventy Stanzas* which is embedded in it.[3]

The colophon to the Peking edition of Candrakīrti's *Shūnyatāsaptativṛtti* indicates that it was translated in India at Nālandā monastery by Abhayākara and Dharma grags. Abhayākara was, according to Ruegg, "one of the last of the great Indian Buddhist masters whose works we possess," and "a prolific polymath" who was "a scholar of the Vikramashīla seminary" and "flourished at the time of King Rāmapāla (rg. ca. 1077-1130)."[4] According to the *Cambridge History of India*, Rāmapāla's reign dates are about 1077 to 1120.[5] Tārānatha states that Abhayākara was upādhyāya ("gatekeeper," actually a title of respect) at both Vikramashīla and Nālandā during the reign of King Rāmapāla.[6] He may have died in 1125 A.D.[7] However, such statements do not mean that Abhayākara lived during the entire period of Rāmapāla's reign; indeed there is evidence to suggest that he lived at the beginning of Rāmapāla's reign, but not the end and that either he did not die in 1125, or else lived an exceedingly long life.

For example, the *Blue Annals* states that Abhayākara was a disciple of Nāropa in the Kālachakra lineage.[8] The date of Nāropa's death is not certain. Guenther suggests 1100 A.D.,[9] while Ferrari suggests 1040 A.D.[10] In the biography of Atīsha we read that Nāropa visited Vikramashīla for about twenty days while Tshul khrims of Nag tsho was there, conversed with Atīsha, and died several days later. We also read that "Some relics of his remains were brought to Tibet by Atīsha."[11] In the biography of Marpa we read of Atīsha meeting Marpa after he had left Vikramashīla and telling Marpa of Nāropa's death.[12] This evidence would suggest that Nāropa died around 1040 A.D. If Abhayākara died in 1125, then he must have received his initiation into the Kālachakra at a very young age and lived to a very ripe old age.

Further evidence comes from several colophons which show Abhayākara and Tshul khrims rgyal ba of Nag tsho as co-translators: Peking Ed. #3965, #3969, #3975, #4012, and #4018. As Tshul khrims rgyal ba spent a few years at Nālandā, invited Atīsha to Tibet and accompanied him to mTho gling, it is clearly the case that Abhayākara was active at Nālandā prior to 1040 A.D., when Atīsha and Tshul khrims departed for Tibet. I can find little further evidence which will help us to pin down Abhayākara's dates, and thus the dates of the translation of the Candrakīrti commentary.[13] Unfortunately, if we look for information about Dharma grags to help us in this matter, we find the yield very scanty.[14] Thus it is impossible to ascertain whether the Candrakīrti commentary to the *Seventy Stanzas* was translated prior to Atīsha's departure for Tibet or posterior to his departure, and thus we also cannot know whether or not such a translation was in the possession of Parahita and gZhon nu mchog at mTho gling monastery, and thus whether the Tibetan translation of the Candrakīrti commentary influenced the translation of Parahita's commentary.

This also implies that although the colophon to the *Seventy Stanzas* lists the names of gZhon nu mchog and Dharma grags, we do not know if one utilized the translation of the other to produce the isolated kārikā(s) of the *Seventy Stanzas*, or if yet a third person utilized their two commentary translations to produce the isolated kārikā(s) of the *Seventy Stanzas*. The third person listed in the *Seventy Stanzas* colophon might seem to be a likely candidate; unfortunately, this third translator, whose name is Khu, is also hard to pin down, as Khu is the name of a clan which produced a number of able translators. Two likely candidates do emerge, however.

Khu ston brtson 'grus byung drung (1011-1075)[15] was born in eastern Tibet, and "conducted extensive studies under Jo bo se btsun" in Khams.[16] He later became a disciple of Atīsha[17] and did some translation work with him.[18] He is also known to have taught the Prajñāpāramitā at Thang po che. It is possible that he is the Khu mentioned in the *Seventy Stanzas* colophon. If so, this is particularly interesting as we have already established that the "auto-commentary" survived the persecution and text destruction of the ninth century, and was thus probably current in eastern Tibet where the practice of Buddhism was maintained.[19] Perhaps Khu ston brought this "autocom-mentary" with him to central Tibet and utilized it, along with the other commentaries, in establishing the edition of the *Seventy Stanzas*? We simply do not have adequate evidence to know.

Moreover, there is a second Khu who is perhaps even a more likely candidate to be the Khu of the *Seventy Stanzas* colophon. The *Blue Annals* indicates that Pa tshab nyi ma grags, who was born in 1055 A.D.,[20] spent twenty three years in India, was active in the early twelfth century as a great expositor of the Mādhyamika system according to Candra-kīrti, and also states that his disciples were responsible for the spread of Mādhyamika in central Tibet.[21] "The great commentary composed by the Acarya Candrakīrti on the *sTong pa nyid bdun cu pa (Shūnyatāsaptati)* has been trans-lated by Abhaya and sNur dharma grags. sPa tshab [sic] with the pandita Mudita revised more than 300 slokas of the first part of this commentary."[22] We know from the col-ophon to *Sūtrasamuccaya* (Tohoku #3934), that a Khu mdo sde 'bar worked with Pa tshab. We also find Khu mdo's name in other colophons to works by Nāgārjuna (for exam-ple, Peking Ed. #5230 and #2666). We also know that Pa tshab prepared translations of Nāgārjuna's *Yuktishashṭikā* and its commentaries, as well as Candrakīrti's *Prasannapa-dā* and *Madhyamakāvatāra*. Perhaps it was Pa tshab's col-league or disciple Khu mdo who, working in Pa tshab's circle of translators, prepared an edition of the *Seventy Stanzas* based on the three available commentaries? We do know that among Pa tshab's "four sons" (i.e., his chief disciples), Zhang thang sag pa founded Thang sag monastery, where he taught Mādhyamika in accordance with Candrakīrti's interpretation. The *Blue Annals* state that "due to him the teaching of the Mādhyamika system continued up to the present time [i.e., 1476 A.D. when composition of the *Blue Annals* began] in Thang sag."[23] The inhabitants of this monastery "which was of great benefit for the Mādhyamika system" include both Candrakīrti and Parahita through Pa tshab in their lineage,[24] which clearly suggests that they had access to both commentaries on the *Seventy Stanzas*.

In the end, there seems inadequate evidence to determine who this Khu mentioned in the *Seventy Stanzas* actually was, nor is the evidence adequate to arrive at a final conclusion about the origin of the edition of the isolated kārikā(s) of the *Seventy Stanzas* in the bsTan 'gyur. Finally, one must even suppose that Bu ston (1290-1364 A.D.), who actually determined which treatises and redactions were to be included in the bsTan 'gyur, might have had a hand in the final editing of the *Seventy Stanzas*. For one thing, the actual original manuscript of the Candrakīrti commentary of Dharma grags (either the Tibetan or the Sanskrit, which one is unclear) was preserved at Bu ston's monastery of Zha lu up until the 1940's.[25] Perhaps, in the end, he compared the versions of the *Seventy Stanzas* in the three commentaries, produced an edited version based on those three, linked the names of the original translators of the differing commentaries in a new colophon, and it is his edition which has come down to us as the *Seventy Stanzas* in the bsTan 'gyur!

The kārikā(s) of the *Seventy Stanzas* do, at any rate, read differently at places than do the kārikā(s) in the commentaries on it, although their meanings generally agree. For the most part the Candrakīrti and Parahita commentaries have quite similar versions of the *Seventy Stanzas* root verses and these are in closer agreement with the isolated root verses of the *Seventy Stanzas* than are the root verses in the "autocommentary." Lindtner, who also notes this, suggests that the latter commentary may have been unknown to those who prepared the former two commentaries, as does Ruegg.[26] The evidence which we have thus far adduced in this chapter would tend to support this conclusion. We are thus left with what appear to be two separate transmissions of the *Seventy Stanzas*. One is represented by the isolated *Seventy Stanzas* kārikā(s) in the bsTan 'gyur, the Candrakīrti commentary and the Parahita commentary, and the other is represented by the "autocommentary." Although the Tibetan version of the "autocommentary" is certainly older than the Tibetan versions of the Candrakīrti and Parahita commentaries, this says nothing about the age of the Sanskrit originals. Finally, we have no clear information which would allow us to date the redaction of the isolated kārikā(s) of the *Seventy Stanzas* in the bsTan 'gyur, although it seems probable that they are based on the Candrakīrti and Parahita commentaries.

There is thus no basis for determining which transmission is derived from the oldest Sanskrit redaction of the *Seventy Stanzas* nor which transmission is the more accurate translation of the lost Sanskrit original. Thus a decision about the most accurate reading for establishing a text edition or translation of the *Seventy Stanzas* is left in the hands of individual contemporary translators who must make such judgements in accordance with other criteria.

Section 3-4 Contemporary Translation Activities

Among Nāgārjuna's treatises, the *Seventy Stanzas* seems not to have aroused too much interest on the part of translators until about the last ten years. No doubt this is due, in part, to the difficulties of the text and its discrepencies in the commentaries, the loss of the Sanskrit original and the assumption that for the most part it merely duplicates arguments made in the *Mula*. As to this assumption, readers who compare the two texts will find that this is not entirely the case, although in both style and content the two treatises are similar enough to assure that they were composed by the same author.

In recent years the *Seventy Stanzas* has been translated into Danish[1] and Japanese.[2] A number of stanzas of the *Seventy Stanzas* have been translated into English in various scholarly articles and popular books.[3] The first complete translation of the *Seventy Stanzas* into English was my own in 1979.[4] In 1981 Luvsantseren published an English translation of the *Seventy Stanzas*[5] which was followed by Lindtner's in 1982.[6] Unfortunately, as Luvsantseren's translation was published in Mongolia I have been unable to obtain a copy.

Lindtner, in commenting on his translation of the *Seventy Stanzas* states "Though I have consulted C[andrakīrti] and P[arahita] my translation of the kārikās strictly follows the svavṛtti [autocommentary] which must, of course, remain the final authority in questions of interpretation."[7] I see no reason why the "autocommentary" should remain "the final authority." As I have shown, the "autocommentary" was translated several centuries prior to the Candrakīrti and Parahita commentaries and independently of them. But this does not mean that it was authored prior to these commentaries, and there is some evidence to suggest that indeed it was not authored prior to them (cf. section 3-1). There also is no certainty that the "autocommentary" was actually authored by Nāgārjuna. It may have been, but it may not have been; in the case of the "autocommentary" on the *Mula (Akutobhayā)* scholarly opinion leans in the direction of refuting the attribution of authorship to Nāgārjuna, as I also have suggested (cf. section 3-1) and as Lindtner suggests.[8] Though the original translation of the "autocommentary" certainly predates the translation of the Candrakīrti and Parahita commentaries as well as the isolated kārikā(s) of the *Seventy Stanzas* in the bsTan 'gyur, there is no reason to assume that any one of the Sanskrit redactions of the *Seventy Stanzas* which were translated and worked into the Tibetan translations of the commentaries was a more faithful copy of the second or third century A.D. original. Nor is there any reason to presume that an earlier translation is more accurate than a later translation. There is thus no reason to presume the superiority of the "autocommentary" as a basis for establishing the text of the *Seventy Stanzas* or for making translations or interpretations. On the other hand, there is also no fundamental reason for not using the "autocommentary" for establishing the text of the *Seventy Stanzas* or for guidance in translating it or interpreting it. As I suggested in section 3-3, the "autocommentary" represents one transmission of the *Seventy Stanzas* while the Candrakīrti and Parahita commentaries represent another. The isolated kārikā(s) of the

Seventy Stanzas in the bsTan 'gyur are probably connected to the Candrakīrti and Parahita transmissions, and were certainly edited after these two commentaries were translated, but the "autocommentary" may also have been consulted by the editor who prepared this redaction of the *Seventy Stanzas*.

My aim in translating and presenting the *Seventy Stanzas* has been to document what the contemporary Tibetan tradition believes Nāgārjuna to be saying, and to place this explication in the framework of the monastic educational curriculum because the texts studied in this curriculum determine the interpretations given to Nāgārjuna. Since this tradition selfconsciously places itself in the lineage which follows Candrakīrti's interpretation of Nāgārjuna, it makes sense to use the Candrakīrti commentary as the basis for making interpretations of the *Seventy Stanzas*.

We have used all the available commentaries and versions of the *Seventy Stanzas* when clarifying obscurities and scribal errors in the Tibetan text of the *Seventy Stanzas*. When discrepencies in the texts have gone beyond this and there has been no other way to establish the best reading of the text we have followed Candrakīrti, both to establish the text and to translate it. In truth I can make no claim that the translation of the *Seventy Stanzas* in this volume is a completely accurate version of what Nāgārjuna was saying when he wrote the *Seventy Stanzas*. There have been too many centuries of copying, editing and interpreting the kārikā(s) for any translator to make such a claim. Moreover, every translator brings certain philosophical assumptions into the activity of translating, and the resultant text bears the stamp of these assumptions. Different assumptions also effect the choice of redactions used as the bases for the translation. As we have followed the Candrakīrti commentary to clarify difficulties in the *Seventy Stanzas* text, our translation of the *Seventy Stanzas* differs in places from Lindtner's, who has followed the "autocommentary." This does not make either translation superior to the other: each is correct in what it translates. One claim that I can make, however, is that our translation is an accurate rendering of what contemporary Tibetans of the dGe lugs pa sect say Nāgārjuna means, and this is all we had in mind.

In a larger cultural sense, however, there is a problem with assuming that English speakers will be able to understand what Tibetans say Nāgārjuna means simply because they say it in English or because I have translated it into English. Concepts like "inherent existence" (svabhāva; rang bzhin) or "emptiness" (shūnyatā, stong pa nyid) or even "permanence" (nityatva, rtag pa nyid) all have special technical meanings in a treatise such as the *Seventy Stanzas*. These are familiar to a Tibetan monk who has engaged in many years of formal study of the various treatises which explain these terms and their significance in the larger Buddhist scriptural context. Most English speakers do not have the benefit of such an education, and so lacking the proper context for understanding the terms in the *Seventy Stanzas*, may misinterpret their meanings. We have sought to minimize this problem by interpolating many words into our translation of the *Seventy Stanzas* which do not appear in the Tibetan text and by providing a stanza by stanza commentary on it. To maintain a distinction between those words which do and do not appear in the Tibetan text, in section 2-2 we have italicized those English words which literally translate words in the Tibetan text, and left our interpolated words without italicization. For the scholar, the Tibetan text is also provided. I have already indicated how we established the text.

To provide a more systematic insight into the scriptural context in which Tibetan monks function when reading Nāgārjuna and to aid the reader in understanding the thrust of the arguments in the *Seventy Stanzas* I have written a chapter which outlines some fundamentals of Buddhist thought (1-2), epistemology (1-3) and psychology (1-4 and 1-5). I have also written a section which summarizes the basic elements of Nāgārjuna's discourse (1-6).

Footnotes

FOOTNOTES, Preface

1. I have discussed this issue and the value of Buddhadharma for the practice of psychotherapy in the west in: Komito, "Tibetan Buddhism and Psychotherapy: A Conversation with the Dalai Lama," and "Tibetan Buddhism and Psychotherapy: Further Conversations with the Dalai Lama."

FOOTNOTES, Section 1-2
1. Majjhima Nikāya, 1.262; Samyutta Nikāya, 2.28.
2. Conze, Buddhist Thought in India, p. 15.
3. Dhammasangani 1309.
4. Segal, "Sleep and The Inner Landscape: An interview with the Tibetan physician Dr. Yeshe Dhonden," p. 31.

FOOTNOTES, Section 1-3
1. Elaborated in Dharmakīrti's Commentary to Ideal Mind, Pramāṇavārttikākārikā, Tshad ma rnam 'grel gyi tshig le'ur byas pa. A complete outline of Dharmakīrti's epistemology can be found in Rabten, The Mind and its Functions. In this section I only discuss those aspects of this epistemol-

ogy that are directly relevant to understanding the *Seventy Stanzas*. This epistemology is also presented, in a somewhat different arrangement, in Akya Yong dzin, *A Compendium of Ways of Knowing* and Rinbochay and Napper, *Mind in Tibetan Buddhism*.
2. Cf. also stanza 62.

FOOTNOTES, Section 1-4
1. Especially Asaṅga's *Compendium of Abhidharma, Abhidharmasamuccaya, mNgon pa kun btus*. Asaṅga's system is summarized in Rabten, *The Mind and its Functions*.
2. Rabten, ibid., p. 52.
3. Ibid.
4. Ibid., p. 59.
5. Ibid., p. 58.

FOOTNOTES, Section 1-5
1. Taken from the *Visuddhimagga* as translated by Conze in *Buddhist Meditation*, p. 113-118. I have substituted the term "dhyāna" for "jhana" throughout.
2. The description of the meditative path is extremely complex, and what follows is a mere thumbnail sketch which, for the sake of brevity, leaves out many important details. A full detailed description of these techniques of meditation can be found in Rinbochay et al., *Meditative States in Tibetan Buddhism*. A detailed description of the path in regards to taking emptiness as the object of meditation can be found in Hopkins, *Meditation on Emptiness*.
3. The Tibetan view is that to obtain this final path one must take up the practice of tantra; cf. Hopkins, ibid., p. 109-123.

FOOTNOTES, Section 1-6
1. Cf. section 1-2 and Hopkins' various discussions of ignorance listed on p. 996 of *Meditation on Emptiness*. Hopkins' book is the most complete exposition of the Tibetan interpretation of Candrakīrti now available in English; it

expounds in detail many of the points I have summarized in this section.

2. *Prasannapadā*, folio 456-7; Sprung, *Lucid Exposition of the Middle Way*, p. 211. Sprung's book is the most complete translation of Candrakīrti's *Prasannapadā* now available in English.

3. *Seventy Stanzas*, stanza 2. Here nirvāṇa refers to "intrinsic" or "natural" nirvāṇa; cf. stanza 63.

FOOTNOTES, *Section 3-1*

1. Hoffmann, *Religions of Tibet*, p. 32.
2. Lindtner, *Nagarjuniana*, p. 9-17.
3. Obermiller, *History of Buddhism*, Vol. I, p. 50.
4. Ibid., p. 51.
5. Obermiller, "The Doctrine of Prajñāpāramitā as Exposed in the Abhisamayālamkāra of Maitreya," *Acta Orientalia*, XI, p. 4.
6. Tsong kha pa, *rTsa she ti ka chen rigs pa'i rgya mtsho*, p. 26-27.
7. Chattopadhyaya, *Tāranatha's History of Buddhism in India*, chapter on Nāgārjuna. Walleser, *Life of Nāgārjuna*, p. 434, as quoted in Robinson, *Early Mādhyamika in India and China*, p. 26.
8. Obermiller, "The Doctrine of Prajñāpāramitā as Exposed in the Abhisamayālamkāra of Maitreya," in *Acta Orientalia* XI, p. 4.
9. Peking Ed. #5344, folio 276b.
10. Peking Ed. #5345, folio 324a.
11. Robinson, *Early Mādhyamika in India and China*, p. 28.
12. Murti, *The Central Philosophy of Buddhism*, p. 89; Lindtner, *Nagarjuniana*, p. 31-33.
13. la Vallée Poussin, *Prasannapadā*, p. 89.
14. Ramanan, *Nāgārjuna's Philosophy*, p. 36.
15. Robinson, *Early Mādhyamika in India and China*, p. 32; Hsueh-li Cheng, *Nāgārjuna's 'Twelve Gate Treatise,'* translates *Seventy Stanzas* stanza 8 on p. 56 and stanza 19 on p. 85, but does not provide the text.

16. Ruegg, *The Literature of The Madhyamaka School of Philosophy in India*, p. 21.

17. Walleser, *Die Mittlere des Nāgārjuna nach der tibetischen version ubertragen.*

18. De Jong, *Cing Chapitres de la Prasannapadā*, p. IX.

19. Lindtner, *Nagarjuniana*, p. 15-16.

20. Murti, *The Central Philosophy of Buddhism*, p. 89.

21. Obermiller, "The Doctrine of Prajñāpāramitā as Exposed in the Abhisamayālamkāra of Maitreya," *Acta Orientalia* XI, p. 4-5.

22. Streng, *Emptiness*, p. 239.

23. Ruegg, *The Literature of the Madhyamaka School of Philosophy in India*, p. 71.

FOOTNOTES, Section 3-2

1. 1953, p. 313.

2. Tucci, *Minor Buddhist Texts*, Part II, p. 52-54.

3. *Journal Asiatique*, 1953, p. 315.

4. Folio 27a, and also Inada, *Nāgārjuna*, p. 188.

5. Hoffmann, *Tibet: A Handbook*, p. 133.

6. Roerich, *The Blue Annals*, p. 45, and also Wayman, *Calming the Mind and Discerning the Real*, p. 5. See also section 3-3 note 19.

7. la Vallée Poussin, *Catalogue of the Tibetan Manuscripts from the India Office Library*, p. 204.

8. Lindtner, *Nagarjuniana*, p. 42-44.

9. Ibid., p. 11.

10. Robinson, *Early Mādhyamika in India and China*, p. 26-27.

11. Hsueh-li Cheng, *Nāgārjuna's 'Twelve Gate Treatise,'* p. 56 and 85.

12. Robinson, *Early Mādhyamika in India and China*, p. 32-33.

13. Lindtner, *Nagarjuniana*, p. 11; Cheng, *Nāgārjuna's 'Twelve Gate Treatise,'* p. 27.

14. Robinson, *Early Mādhyamika in India and China*, p. 72.

15. Inada, *Nāgārjuna*, p. 191.

FOOTNOTES, Section 3-3
1. Peking Ed. #5344, folio 276b.
2. Das, *Journal of the Buddhist Text Society*, p. 29.
3. See Komito, *A Study of Nāgārjuna's 'Śūnyatā-saptati-kārikā-nāma,'* p. 33-36 for further details concerning Parahita and gZhon nu mchog.
4. Ruegg, "The gotra, ekayāna and tathāgatagarbha theories of the Prajñāpāramitā according to Dharmamitra and Abhayākaragupta," in *Prajñāpāramitā and Related Systems*, p. 284.
5. Vol. III, p. 511.
6. Chattopadhyaya, *Tāranatha's History of Buddhism in India*, p. 329.
7. "According to Sum pa Ye shes dpal 'byor('s) Re'u mig Abhayākaragupta died in shin sbrul = 1125." Ruegg, *The Literature of the Madhyamaka School of Philosophy in India*, p. 114.
8. Roerich, *The Blue Annals*, p. 760.
9. *The Life and Teaching of Nāropa*, Introduction.
10. Ibid., note 2.
11. Das, "Indian Pandits in Tibet," in *Journal of the Buddhist Text and Research Society*, Vol. I, part 1, p. 21.
12. Bacot, *La Vie de Marpa*, p. 34.
13. See Komito, *A Study of Nāgārjuna's 'Śūnyatā-saptati-kārikā-nāma,'* p. 36-43 for more information on Abhayākara.
14. Ibid., p. 43-44.
15. Roerich, *The Blue Annals*, p. 93-94 and p. 404.
16. Ibid., p. 93.
17. Chattopadhyaya, *Atīsha and Tibet*, p. 363.
18. Cf. colophon to Peking Ed. #5028.
19. "In his [rNgog lo tsa ba blo ldan shes rab, born 1059 A.D.] teaching he followed the traditions of the Prajñāpāramitā as taught during the period of the early spread of the Doctrine and which had been preserved in Khams." Roerich, *The Blue Annals*, p. 328 and p. 330.
20. Ruegg, *The Literature of the Madhyamaka School of*

Philosophy in India, p. 114.
21. Roerich, *The Blue Annals*, p. 341-343.
22. Ibid., p. 342.
23. Ibid., p. 344-45.
24. Ibid., p. 344.
25. Ibid., p. 342.
26. Lindtner, *Nagarjuniana*, p. 32; Ruegg, *The Literature of the Madhyamaka School of Philosophy in India*, p. 20.

FOOTNOTES, Section 3-4
1. Lindtner, *Nāgārjuna's Filosofiske Voerker*, 1982.
2. Uryuzu, *Daijo Butten* XIV.
3. Dalai Lama XIV and Hopkins, *The Buddhism of Tibet and the Key to the Middle Way*, 1975, translates *Seventy Stanzas* 5ab on p. 69 and stanza 64 on p. 75. Wayman, *Calming the Mind and Discerning the Real*, 1978, translates stanza 1 on p. 276 and stanza 68 on p. 195. Ruegg, *The Literature of the Madhyamaka School of Philosophy in India*, 1981, translates stanzas 58, 69, 70, 71 and 72 on p. 21. Cheng, *Nāgārjuna's 'Twelve Gates Treatise,'* 1982, translates stanza 19 from the Chinese on p. 85 and apparently, though there is no formal attribution to this effect, stanza 8 on p. 56.
4. Komito, *A Study of Nāgārjuna's 'Śūnyatā-saptati-kārikā-nāma,'* 1979.
5. Luvsantseren, *Philosophical Views of Nāgārjuna*, 1981. Reviewed in *Buddhists for Peace, Journal of the Asian Buddhist Conference for Peace*, Vol. 3 (1981), p. 63.
6. Lindtner, *Nagarjuniana*, 1982.
7. Ibid., p. 32-33.
8. Ibid., p. 15-16.

Bibliography

Entries under "Peking Edition" refer to *The Tibetan Tripi-taka*, D.T. Suzuki, ed. Tokyo: Otani University, 1962.

Akya Yong dzin. *Blo rigs kyi sdom tshig blang dor gsal ba'i me long.* Translated by Geshe Ngawang Dhargyey et al. as *A Compendium of Ways of Knowing.* Dharamsala: Library of Tibetan Works and Archives, 1976.

Asaṅga. *Compendium of Abhidharma. Abhidharmasamuc-caya, mNgon pa kun btus.* Peking Edition #550.

Atīsha. *Bodhipathapradīpa, Byang chub lam gyi sgron ma* and *Bodhimārgapradīpapañjikā, Byang chub lam gyi sgron ma'i dka' 'grel.* Text in Sherburne, Richard F. *A Study of Atīśa's 'Commentary' on His 'Lamp of the Enlightenment Path.'* Ann Arbor: University Microfilms International, 1976.

Bacot, Jacques. *La Vie de Marpa le "Traducteur."* Paris: Buddhica 1, 7, 1937.

Buddhaghosa, Bhadantācariya. *Visuddhimagga.* Selections translated by Conze, Edward in *Buddhist Meditation.* New York: Harper and Row, 1969.

216

Candrakīrti. *Mūlamadhyamakavṛttiprasannapadā, dbU ma rtsa ba'i 'grel pa tshig gsal ba.* Peking Edition #5260.

Candrakīrti. *Shūnyatāsaptativṛtti, sTong pa nyid bdun cu pa'i 'grel pa.* Peking Edition #5268

Chattopadhyaya, Alaka. *Atīśa and Tibet.* Calcutta: Indian Studies, 1967.

Chattopadhyaya, D. *Tārānatha's History of Buddhism in India.* Simla: Indian Institute of Advanced Study, 1970.

Cheng, Hsueh-li. *Nāgārjuna's 'Twelve Gates Treatise.'* Dordrecht: Reidel, 1982.

Conze, Edward. *Buddhist Thought in India.* Ann Arbor: University of Michigan Press, 1973.

Das, Sarat C. "Indian Pandits in Tibet," *Journal of the Buddhist Text and Research Society,* Calcutta. Vol. I, part 1, 1893.

De Jong, J. W. *Cing Chapitres de la Prasannapadā.* Paris: Librarie Orientaliste Paul Geuthner, 1949.

Dhammasangani. Translated by Caroline Rhys Davids as *A Buddhist Manual of Psychological Ethics.* New Delhi: Oriental Books Reprint Corporation, 1975.

Dharmakīrti. *Commentary to Ideal Mind, Pramāṇavārttikakārikā, Tshad ma rnam 'grel gyi tshig le'ur byas pa.* Peking Edition #5709.

Guenther, Herbert. *The Life and Teaching of Naropa.* London: Oxford University Press, 1974.

Gyatso, Tenzin: The Fourteenth Dalai Lama. *The Buddhism of Tibet and the Key to the Middle Way.* New York: Harper and Row, 1975.

Hoffmann, Helmut. *Religions of Tibet.* London: Allen and Unwin, 1961.

Hoffmann, Helmut. *Tibet: A Handbook.* Bloomington: Research Center for the Language Sciences, 1975.

Hopkins, Jeffrey. *Meditation on Emptiness.* London: Wisdom Publications, 1983.

Inada, Kenneth. *Nāgārjuna: Mūlamadhyamakakārikā.* Tokyo: Hokuseido Press, 1970.

Komito, David. *A Study of Nāgārjuna's 'Śūnyatā-saptati-*

kārikā-nāma.' Ann Arbor: University Microfilms International, 1979.

Komito, David. "Tibetan Buddhism and Psychotherapy: A Conversation with the Dalai Lama," *The Journal of Transpersonal Psychology*, Vol. XV, #1, 1983.

Komito, David. "Tibetan Buddhism and Psychotherapy: Further Conversations with the Dalai Lama," *The Journal of Transpersonal Psychology*, Vol. XVI, #1, 1984.

la Vallée Poussin, Louis de. *Mūlamadhyamakakārikās de Nāgārjuna avec la Prasannapadā.* St. Petersberg, 1903-1914.

la Vallée Poussin, Louis de. *Catalogue of the Tibetan Manuscripts from the India Office Library.* London: Oxford University Press, 1962.

Lalou, Marcelle. "Les Textes Bouddhiques au Temps du Roi Khri-srong lde-bcan," *Journal Asiatique*, 1953.

Lindtner, Chr. *Nāgārjuna's Filosofiske Voerker.* Copenhagen: (publisher unknown), 1982.

Lindtner, Chr. *Nagarjuniana.* Copenhagen: Akademisk Forlag, 1982.

Luvsantseren, S. *Philosophical Views of Nāgārjuna.* (publisher unknown), 1981.

Majjhima Nikāya. Selections translated in David Kalupahana. *Buddhist Philosophy: A Historical Analysis.* Honolulu: University Press of Hawaii, 1976.

May, Jacques. *Candrakīrti Prasannapadā Madhyamakavṛtti.* Paris: Adrien Maisonneuve, 1959.

Murti, Tirupattur. *The Central Philosophy of Buddhism.* London: Allen and Unwin, 1970.

Nāgārjuna. *Shūnyatāsaptatikārikānāma, sTong pa nyid bdun cu pa'i tshig le'ur byas pa zhes bya ba.* Peking Edition #5227.

Nāgārjuna. *Shūnyatāsaptativṛtti, sTong pa nyid bdun cu pa'i 'grel pa.* Peking Edition #5231.

Obermiller, Eugene. "The Doctrine of Prajñāpāramitā as Exposed in the Abhisamayālamkāra of Maitreya," *Acta Orientalia*, XI, 1932.

Obermiller, Eugene. *History of Buddhism by Bu-ston.* Suzuki Research Foundation (no date given).

Parahita(bhadra). *Shūnyatāsaptativivṛtti, sTong pa nyid bdun cu pa'i rnam par bshad pa.* Peking Edition #5269.

Rabten, Geshé. *The Mind and its Functions.* Mt. Pelerin: Tharpa Choeling, 1981.

Ramanan, K. Venkata. *Nāgārjuna's Philosophy as Presented in the Mahā-Prajñāpāramitā-Śāstra.* Rutland: Tuttle, 1960.

Rinbochay, Lati and Napper, Elizabeth. *Mind in Tibetan Buddhism.* Valois: Gabriel Press, 1980.

Rinbochay, Lati, et al. *Meditative States in Tibetan Buddhism.* London: Wisdom Publications, 1983.

Robinson, Richard. *Early Mādhyamika in India and China.* Madison: University of Wisconsin Press, 1967.

Roerich, George N. *The Blue Annals.* Delhi: Banarsidass, 1976.

Ruegg, David S. "The gotra, ekayāna and tathāgatagarbha theories of the Prajñāpāramitā according to Dharmamitra and Abhayākaragupta," in *Prajñāpāramitā and Related Systems,* Louis Lancaster, ed. Korea: Berkeley Buddhist Studies Series, 1977.

Ruegg, David S. *The Literature of the Madhyamaka School of Philosophy in India.* Wiesbaden: Harrassowitz, 1981.

Samyutta Nikāya. Selections translated in David Kalupahana. *Buddhist Philosophy: A Historical Analysis.* Honolulu: University Press of Hawaii, 1976.

Segal, William and Segal, Marielle. "Sleep and The Inner Landscape: An interview with the Tibetan physician Dr. Yeshe Dhonden," *Parabola,* Vol. VII, #1, 1982.

Sprung, Mervyn. *Lucid Exposition of the Middle Way.* London: Routledge, 1979.

Streng, Frederick. *Emptiness — A Study in Religious Meaning.* New York: Abingdon, 1967.

Tsong kha pa. *rTsa she ti ka chen rigs pa'i rgya mtsho.* Varanasi: Pleasure of Elegant Sayings Press, 1973.

Tucci, Giuseppe. *Minor Buddhist Texts,* Part II. Rome:

Serie Orientale Roma, 1958.

Uryuzu, Ryushin. *Daijo Butten* XIV. (publisher unknown).

Walleser, Max. *Die Mittlere des Nāgārjuna nach der tibetis-chen version ubertragen.* Heidelberg, 1911.

Walleser, Max. "The Life of Nāgārjuna from Tibetan and Chinese Sources," *Hirth Anniversary Volume*, Bruno Schindler, ed. London: Probsthain, (no date given).

Wayman, Alex. *Calming the Mind and Discerning the Real.* New York: Columbia University Press, 1978.

Index

Abhayākara 201
Abhidharma 53, 97
action 56, 145–157
agent 150–151, 154–155
aggregates 27, 33
aggregation 102
analytic meditation 62
— see also meditation
annihilationist view 129
— see also extreme view
appearances 66, 69, 71, 120, 132
appearing object 40, 57, 66
— see also object
appreciation 55
Arhat 101
arising 98, 105–107, 125, 127
— see also dependent arising
arising, enduring, ceasing 125–143
Ārya 56, 58, 64, 174
Asaṅga 52, 66
aspiration 55
Atīsha 188, 199
attention 52, 55, 56
attraction 31
auditory consciousness 37
— see also consciousness

basis of imputation 98, 119, 154
— see also functional basis
— see also imputation

becoming 26, 29
birth 26
birth and death 30
body 37, 148–151
Bu ston 187
Buddha 23–24, 97, 156
buddhahood 65

calm abiding 63
Candrakīrti 157, 177, 189, 202
cause 102, 107, 138
— see also dependent arising
— see also result
cause-effect relationships 25, 107, 129–131, 138–139
cessation 125, 127, 135
cognition 37
— see also conceptual cognition
— see also deceived cognition
— see also direct valid cognition
— see also erroneous cognition
— see also erroneous conceptual cognition
— see also ideal cognition
— see also mistaken conceptual cognition
— see also mistaken sensory cognition
— see also perceptual cognition
— see also perfect cognition

221

— see also valid cognition
— see also valid conceptual cognition
— see also valid perceptual cognition
compassion 181
composite phenomenon 142–144, 149
— see also phenomenon
composite thing 105
— see also thing
compounded phenomenon 104
— see also phenomenon
concentration 55, 56
— see also eight stages of concentration
— see also meditation
conception 36, 42, 50, 154
— see also extreme conception
conception of self 147
— see also self
concepts 37, 66
conceptual cognition 41, 43
— see also cognition
condition 102
— see also dominant condition
— see also immediate condition
— see also object condition
consciousness 26, 30, 37–38, 52, 152, 164, 168–169, 172
— see also auditory consciousness
— see also gustatory consciousness
— see also mental consciousness
— see also olfactory consciousness
— see also primary consciousness
— see also tactile consciousness
— see also visual consciousness
consciousness limb 26, 52
consciousness skandha 38
contact 26–28, 37, 55, 166–168
continuity 130
— see also moment
conventional 146, 153, 178
— see also truth

conventional existence 99, 156
— see also existence
conventional "I" 100
— see also "I"
— see also self
conventional terms 178
— see also worldy convention
conventional truth 65, 71, 178–179
— see also truth
correct belief 47–48, 62, 67
craving 26, 28
cyclic existence 31

death, grief, suffering 26
— see also suffering
deceived cognition 43
— see also cognition
defined 137
definition 137
delusion 31, 150
dependence 28, 120
dependent arising
— see dependence
— see also dependent origination
dependent origination 25, 110–121, 172–178
devoid of inherent existence 69, 102
— see also empty of inherent existence
Dharma 180
Dharma grags 181, 201
Dharmakīrti 36, 50, 67
direct valid cognition 48
— see also cognition
discernment 55–56
discernment without signs 56–57
disintegration 127
— see also momentary disintegration
distinctions 140
distorted traces 31
distortions 112, 124, 170, 172
"does not exist" 69, 156
— see also existence
"does not exist inherently" 70
— see also existence

dominant condition 38
— see also condition

ear 37
eight stages of concentration 59
— see also concentration
emanation 154
empty (emptiness) 62–65, 68–70, 102, 133, 176–178
— see also inherent existence
— see also truth
empty of inherent existence 69
— see also devoid of inherent existence
— see also empty
— see also existence
enduring 127
entrances
— see sense fields
epistemology 37
erroneous cognition 44
— see also cognition
erroneous conceptual cognition 41
— see also cognition
eternalism 134, 175, 177, 180
eternalist extreme 157
eternalist view 129
— see also extreme view
existence 69, 99, 156
— see also conventional existence
— see also devoid of inherent existence
— see also "does not exist"
— see also "does not exist inherently"
— see also empty
— see also empty of inherent existence
— see also exists non-inherently
— see also inherent existence
— see also non-inherent existence
— see also true existence
existence and non-existence 103–104, 125–129, 144–145
"exists-and-does-not-exist"156
exists non-inherently 70

experience 151
extinction 134
extreme conception 170
— see also conception
extreme view 73, 157
— see also annihilationist view
— see also eternalist view
— see also nihilistic view
— see also overestimation
— see also underestimation
eye 37

feeling 26–27, 55, 138–139, 167
five aggregates 153
— see also aggregates
form 157–167
four evil preconceptions
— see distortions
four great elements 32, 158–159
four noble truths 31
functional basis 141
— see also basis of imputation
functional phenomenon 68, 123, 126
— see also phenomenon
functional thing 68, 99, 175
— see also thing

gateways
— see sense fields
general examination 55, 57
generic image
— see mental image
grasping 26, 28
grasping at self 100
— see also self
gustatory consciousness 37
— see also consciousness
gZhon nu mchog 182, 200

"I" 29, 33, 99–100
— see also conventional "I"
ideal cognition 44
— see also cognition
ignorance 26, 30, 114–117, 172, 175–176
immediate condition 38
— see also condition
impermanence 170

— see also permanence
imputation 50, 66, 70–71, 98
— see also basis of imputation
— see also superimposition
imputation by thought 153
inattentive perception 46
— see also perception
individuality 102–103
infallible 45
inference 45
inherent existence 68–69, 99, 102
— see also devoid of inherent
    existence
— see also empty
— see also empty of inherent
    existence
— see also existence
inherently existing characteristics
    50, 113
initial moment 40
— see also moment
innate conception of inherent ex-
    istence 64
— see also existence
intelligence/wisdom 55–56
intention 55–56, 157

karmic formations 26, 30
Khu 182, 202–204

lDan kar catalog 192
liberation 132–133, 135, 152, 172
— see also peace

main mind 116
— see also mind
Manjushrī 97
mark 110
— see also sign
meditation 59, 173
— see also analytic meditation
— see also concentration
mental consciousness 37, 39, 152
— see also consciousness
— see also mind
mental factors 116
— see also secondary mental fac-
    tors

mental (generic) image 40, 42, 50,
    63, 156
mental image of emptiness 63, 178
middle way 179
mind 37–38, 160–162
— see also main mind
— see also mental consciousness
— see also moments of mind
— see also unmistaken mind
mistaken conceptual cognition 47,
    62
— see also cognition
— see also conception
mistaken sensory perception 46
— see also perception
moment 37
— see also initial moment
momentary disintegration 132, 143
— see also disintegration
moments of mind 111, 162
— see also mind
Mula
— see *Mūlamadhyamakakārikā*
Mūlamadhyamakakārikā 181, 186
mutually dependent 137, 139

Nāgārjuna 17, 67–74, 156, 185–
    187
name and form 26–27, 29, 32
name 32
nihilism 175, 177
nihilistic view 134, 157, 179
— see also extreme view
nirvāṇa
— see peace
non-composite phenomenon 142,
    144
— see also phenomenon
non-existing 99
— see also existence
non-functional phenomenon 123,
    126
— see also phenomenon
non-functional thing 99, 175
— see also thing
non-inherent existence 70, 74, 176
— see also existence
nose 37

object 66, 120
— see also appearing object
object condition 38, 68
— see also condition
olfactory consciousness 37
— see also consciousness
omniscience 65
— see also truth
origination
— see dependent origination
overestimation 73, 129, 147, 170
— see also extreme view

Parahita 177, 189, 200
path of accumulation 174
path of meditation 64
path of no more learning 65
path of preparation 64, 174
path of seeing 49, 64, 133, 174
peace 31, 35, 101, 132–136, 155, 175, 180–181
— see also liberation
perception 36
— see also inattentive perception
— see also mistaken sensory perception
— see also valid direct perception
— see also valid perceptual cognition
perceptual cognition 41
— see also cognition
perfect cognition 44
— see also cognition
perfect reason
— see inference
permanence 129
— see also impermanence
person 32–36, 74, 99, 104, 151
— see also conventional "I"
— see also self
phenomenon 68, 72, 124
— see also composite phenomenon
— see also functional phenomenon
— see also non-functional phenomenon
— see also produced and compounded phenomena
— see also thing

Prasannapadā 157, 189
precise analysis 55, 57
preconceptions 171
— see also distortions
primary consciousness 38, 53
— see also consciousness
produced and compounded phenomena 104
— see also phenomenon

Ratnāvalī 181
reason 160
— see also inference
rebirth 29, 35
— see also liberation
recollection 55
regret 55
result 103, 107, 138
— see also cause
— see also cause-effect relationships
revulsion 31

secondary mental factors 38, 53
— see also mental factors
seeing 139
— see also sense fields
self 69, 175
— see also conception of self
— see also conventional "I"
— see also grasping at self
— see also person
— see also selflessness
self-existent 165
selflessness 32–35, 49
— see also person
self-sufficient 74
sense-fields 26–27, 165–166
Seventy Stanzas
— see *Shūnyatāsaptatikārikā-nāma*
Seventy Stanzas Explaining How Phenomena Are Empty of Inhe-

rent Existence
— see *Shūnyatāsaptatikārikā-nāma*
Seventy Stanzas on Emptiness
— see *Shūnyatāsaptatikārikā-nāma*
Shūnyatāsaptatikārikānāma 12–14, 79, 96, 200, 208–210
Shūnyatāsaptativivṛtti 189, 200
Shūnyatāsaptativṛtti 189, 200–201
sign 56, 109
— see also mark
simultaneously 118
six sense fields
— see sense fields
skandha
— see aggregates
sleep 55
smells 37
sounds 37
special insight 63
subsequent moments 40
— see also moment
suchness 152
suffering 148
— see also death, grief, suffering
— see also liberation
superimposition 49, 170
— see also imputation
Sūtra Piṭaka 161
Sūtrasamuccaya 181

tactile consciousness 37
— see also consciousness
tangibles 37
tastes 37
Tathāgata 152, 179
thing 68
— see also composite thing
— see also functional thing
— see also non-functional thing
— see also phenomemon
thought-consciousness 172
— see also consciousness
three poisons 31
three times 107, 140
time
— see three times
tongue 37
true existence 99, 125, 175
— see also existence
truth
— see conventional truth
— see two truths
— see ultimate truth
Tsong kha pa 187
Tun-huang manuscripts 194–197
twelve limbs of dependent origination 26–32
— see also dependent origination
Twelve Topic Treatise 189, 197–198
two truths 65
— see also truth

ultimate 146, 173
— see also truth
ultimate analysis 153
ultimate reality 178
— see also ultimate truth
ultimate truth 65, 71
— see also truth
underestimation 129
— see also extreme view
unmistaken mind 173
— see also cognition
— see also mind

valid cognition 41, 44–45, 67, 116
— see also cognition
valid conceptual cognition 44, 48, 50, 62
— see also cognition
valid direct perception 178
— see also perception
valid perceptual cognition 44
— see also cognition
— see also perception
visual consciousness 37
— see also consciousness

ways of knowing 52
wisdom
— see intelligence/wisdom
worldly convention 97–99
— see also conventional terms